REASONS OF THE HEART

Hourglass Books are for all who long for reformation and revival within the evangelical community. As "tracts for the times" they raise major issues of the day. Each book is serious in tone and probing in style but practical rather than academic, more often a first word than the last. Designed not only to be read but discussed and acted on, Hourglass Books are for all who seek to restore the gospel to evangelicals and evangelicals to the gospel.

Books in the series:

REASONS OF THE HEART

RECOVERING CHRISTIAN PERSUASION

WILLIAM EDGAR

HOURGLASS BOOKS

BAKER BOOK HOUSE

Grand Rapids, Michigan 49516

First printing, June 1996
Second printing, March 1997

Printed in the United States of America

Library of Congress Cataloging-in-Publication Data

Edgar, William.
    Reasons of the heart : recovering Christian persuasion / William Edgar.
      p. cm.
    Includes bibliographical references
    ISBN 0-8010-5138-X (paper)
    1. Witness bearing (Christianity) 2. Persuasion (Psychology)
    p3. Evangelistic work. 4. Apologetics. I. Title.
    BV4520.E34   1996
    248´.5—dc20   96-19575

For information about academic books, resources for Christian leaders, and all new releases available from Baker Book House, visit our web site:
http://www.bakerbooks.com

To Pierre and Hélène Courthial

Whose radiant faith is the best apologetic.

CONTENTS

ACKNOWLEDGMENTS

THIS BOOK, though of modest size, represents the efforts of a number of people beside the author. First and foremost I would like to thank Amy Boucher for her skilled and tireless work as editor. She accomplished the rare goal of greatly improving the manuscript without infringing on my thoughts or style. I am deeply grateful.

I also want to thank the Trinity Forum for the splendid ways I have been encouraged in my field. It has been a rare privilege to work with Os Guinness in the actual front lines of apologetic work.

Judy Parnell of Westminster Seminary deserves special mention, because she devoted a good deal of her own time helping me with word processors and technical matters during the various stages of the writing process.

Finally, I want to thank my family, and especially Barbara, for "being there" during every part of the work in progress. Only those who have had it know how precious this kind of support is.

It is my hope that all concerned will find evidence of their devoted assistance throughout the finished product.

INTRODUCTION

THE CREDIBILITY GAP

> Modern culture is not altogether opposed to the
> gospel. But it is out of all connection with it. It not
> only prevents the acceptance of Christianity. It
> prevents Christianity even from getting a hearing.
> —J. Gresham Machen,*What Is Christianity?*, 1951

THE HOUR OF APOLOGETICS

I'LL NEVER FORGET A CONVERSATION I had with a relative of mine
shortly after I became a Christian. Being excited about my new-
found faith (to say the least) and wanting to share with my family
what I had discovered, I challenged him with the Bible's claims,
the reality of Christ's presence, and the hope of heaven. Not too
far into the conversation, he asked me what real difference becoming a Christian would make in his life. His question brought me up
short. I wanted to tell him he would be a better person, but he
was one of the best people I knew, without apparent needs. I
wanted to say that he would have new meaning in his life, but
that seemed trivial to a man who had a good job, a loving family, and no particular anguish about the larger issues of life. Everything I thought of sounded inconsequential. I couldn't connect.

Persuading our generation about deep issues is becoming
more and more difficult as our culture moves away from certain
shared assumptions and values. And today it is not only Christians who feel impotent sharing their deepest convictions. What-

ever issue espoused, often the day is carried not by those who attempt the kind of persuasion that depends on careful reasoning and integrity, but by a power play such as rage or the more subtle tyranny of the expert. In this atmosphere, many Christians whose convictions are strong and whose faith is foundational are understandably frustrated. Different barriers are raised. Air-tight arguments fall on deaf ears.

In short, the Christian message seems *irrelevant*—followers of Christ have wonderful answers to questions people seem not to be asking. We feel like someone selling the latest, most efficient equipment for doing alchemy. The sales pitch may be as good as the wares, but no one is interested because no one practices alchemy.

This is the climate into which the hour of apologetics has arrived. Although commending the faith may be difficult, it is crucial for the survival of the church and the spread of the truth. We long to make an impact and a difference in our society, but are faced with a credibility gap between the gospel of Christ and our culture. Every age experiences this tension, yet at the dawn of the twenty-first century the distance seems greater between the message and the audience than previously. Why is this so?

It is partly, no doubt, because Christians have grown so used to their own language, terms, and culture that they have become isolated from those who surround them. A great British preacher used to tell his congregation that the interests dearest to the hearts of believers are peripheral to unbelievers, and that the things most important to unbelievers are insignificant to followers of Christ. He was describing what he considered normal and good. But how healthy is it for Christians and non-Christians to live in such different worlds?

This credibility gap between believers and skeptics is often highlighted for me in church. Occasionally in the Sunday service I try to imagine a particular friend beside me in the pew. What impact would the sermon have on Michael, my Jewish neighbor? Or on the beer-drinking sports fan I met at a baseball game with his sports outlook, "Life is short, play hard"? Or on Mr. Mukerji, a visiting Hindu friend who delighted the children with stories of his travels and who considers his religion an accident of birth? What would church mean to these people, with its "language of Zion"? What would they make of the issues that are so real to me, a Christian, but are undoubtedly foreign to their world?

These questions lead to deeper questions: Why should Christians persuade others about what they believe? Is it not better to live and let live, to be quiet and unobtrusive? Is it ethical to disturb someone else's views with a challenge from religion? Is there not something indecent about apologetics, the defense of the faith?

Indeed these are serious issues. Along this line, one of the most influential theologians of the twentieth century, Karl Barth (1886–1968), believed that Christian apologetics was an illegitimate pursuit. He taught that God should spread his truth directly, without recourse to the complexities of human arguments. Apologetics, in his view, reduced the gospel to the level of human religion, thus spoiling the wonder of God's grace.

Barth's ideas prevailed in the seminaries and pulpits in many parts of the Christian world. Even today, years after his death, apologetics is a neglected discipline in these circles. Did he have a point? Certainly. One tradition in apologetics does reduce the gospel to a cold, human construction. Endless debates about science and faith, proofs for the existence of God, and speculations about the Trinity have often been a distraction, rather than a commendation, for the faith.

Such a radical dismissal, however, falters on two grounds. First, apologetics is commanded in Scripture. Christians are told to be ready to give answers to those who ask why they believe (1 Peter 3:15). For reasons we do not entirely understand, God has entrusted to us the task of heralding his truth. Second, apologetics—the defense of the faith—is impossible to avoid. Ironically, it takes apologetics to discredit apologetics. Barth himself wrote reams and reams of polemical theology.

BALANCING MIND AND HEART

There are at least two other key reasons for Christian apologetics. One is that it provides food for starving people. If what Christians believe is true, then human beings are not innocently going about their business but are in desperate need of answers. To use a time-honored image, Christians are like beggars who have found food and are eager to share it with others. As such, apologetics has a deeply human side that is concerned with the whole person; it is not just a series of dry techniques or rational proofs.

The other reason is that it brings honor to God. The concept of honor is eclipsed in Western society; today the word makes us think of knights in armor and the courtly love of bygone days. But honor is a precious Christian principle that means esteem, homage, and reverence where it is due—supremely, to the Lord.

If what we mean by Christian apologetics is anything less than this, then Karl Barth is right. But there is a better way. Blaise Pascal (1623–1662), the French mathematician, scientist, and theologian, provides the antidote to cold, rationalist apologetics in his *Pensées*. In this anthology of apologetic reflections, he pleads for a proper balance between mind and heart: "We know the truth not only through our reason but also through our heart," he declared to a complacent audience. This is because, to quote his best-known saying, "The heart has its reasons of which reason knows nothing."[1]

It is crucial not to be misled here, for Pascal is not saying that faith is irrational. Rather he is drawing a distinction between the contrived reasonings of the excessively rational apologetics of seventeenth-century philosopher René Descartes and the affections of the heart for another person, particularly God.

In the context of Pascal's writings, his balance is impressive. Reason is good and necessary as long as it knows how to submit to the truth. To do that, it needs the heart's right disposition. The heart, as Pascal puts it, does have its *reasons*. But a system of dry rationalism alone will never lead to God.

DON'T APOLOGIZE

Apologetics, it must be said, is not exactly a household word today. People confuse it with apologizing or being sorry about something, which is actually the opposite of what it means. Arguments could be made to eliminate the word and substitute something else, but few good candidates exist. "Defense of the faith" is an accurate summary of parts of the apologetic enterprise, for the gospel often needs to be set off from hostile criticism. And yet defense is not the only task; a more positive sense is also involved. Perhaps "commending the faith" is better, sounding more congenial. But that term is somewhat genteel and even timid. "Vindicating the faith" is another option. Still, that may sound somewhat belligerent.

With no great issue at stake, it is best to stay with *apologetics* and offer an explanation. The word actually has a noble pedigree. The root meaning of the Greek term is judicial and might accurately be translated, "getting oneself off a charge." Apologetics breaks down into *apo*, which is a preposition meaning (in this case) "unto," and *logos*. *Logos* in Greek has a rich meaning, primary referring to the "word," the word by which the inward thought is expressed. But it also signifies the thought process itself, or "reason."

Reasoning is a varied function that may involve conversation, discourse, reports, or a story. The central kind of reasoning done in apologetics is argument, which means to marshal evidence in support of a person or position. The methods of persuasion used in an argument may be diverse, as long as they all help to present convincing reasons in defense of a point of view. Apologetics, whether Christian or not, then, means to argue a case in favor of a person or a position. It carries the primary connotation of defense.

One of the most famous ancient examples of such a defense is Plato's *Apology*. In this philosophical masterpiece Plato reports on the defense Socrates gives when charged and tried with three crimes: introducing new divinities to Athens, denying the official gods of the state, and corrupting young men. Socrates appeals in his moving speech from his conscience to the truth, attempting in vain to be released from the accusations. He employs what has come to be known as the Socratic method, an approach in which one asks a series of questions, leading the adversary down a certain path. After the questioning has evoked just the desired answers, the opponent becomes disarmed.

The Socratic method is called a dialectical approach because it engages in dialogue with a generous use of irony and paradox to penetrate deeply into the issues. Socrates often used storytelling as well. Today this method is still used in law schools for good reason; the ancient dialectical approach has much in common with a legal mind.

Many examples of this kind of defense can be found in secular literature. One of the best known writings from the late Renaissance is Michel De Montaigne's *Apologie de Raymond Sebond*. Penned shortly after the St. Bartholomew's Day massacre of the Huguenots (1572), it stresses not the sufficiency but the utter vanity of human reason. Our knowledge is always tentative, constantly changing, prone to pride. Montaigne's biting irony, coupled with his great knowledge of the classics, is so inspiring that we still profit from his reasoning today.

In the Christian context apologetics has a special meaning. For two thousand years the defense of the faith has been the mission of the church. It has, of course, taken many different shapes and stemmed from many different versions of how apologetics works. But down through the centuries this discipline has been considered a necessary and urgent task for believers who are faced with unbelief.

It could not be otherwise, for the Christian faith claims to be true. Whatever else may be said, a distinction between truth and error has always been fundamental to the church. Different apologies, or statements of the truth, were developed to vindicate the Christian position and defend the faith against various attacks. Opposition to belief may be openly hostile or more subtle, but is a fact that requires the practice of apologetics.

AN APPEAL TO THE HEART'S REASONS

This book is an "apology for apologetics" of the Pascalian sort. Part one lays the foundations for apologetics. Chapters one and two describe both some obstacles and opportunities for recovering Christian persuasion today. Although our age is no different from any other in terms of the basic issues, we face specific challenges, such as the claims of the postmodern condition. In chapters three and four we will move to the biblical basis for the task of apologetics, showing the various ways in which the Scriptures not only authorize but mandate responsible persuasion. The fifth chapter, drawing on the first four, focuses on method as it sets forth the principles behind actual arguments in favor of the Christian position.

In the second part we will more specifically treat various questions that arise in apologetic discussions, giving suggestions for responding. Chapter six deals with barriers to belief, probing the question: "Why do people resist considering the most basic questions about life?"

Then we will explore three major issues that often surface in discussions about faith. The first, in chapter seven, is whether religion is an illusion. Chapter eight looks at the second, the matter of the uniqueness of the Christian faith. And chapter nine is concerned with the third, the problem of evil.

Finally, chapter ten treats the subject of assurance, its necessity and limits. Although none of this is exhaustive, the book is designed to encourage the reader to engage in Christian persuasion, appealing to the heart's reasons.

Part One

FOUNDATIONS

TODAY'S UNUSUAL OPPORTUNITY

To know and to serve God, of course, is why we're here, a clear truth that, like the nose on your face, is near at hand and easily discernible but can make you dizzy if you try to focus on it hard. But a little faith will see you through. What else will do *except* faith in such a cynical, corrupt time? When the country goes temporarily to the dogs, cats must learn to be circumspect, walk on fences, sleep in trees, and have faith that all this woofing is not the last word.

—Garrison Keillor, Lake Wobegon Radio Show

No Golden Age

COMMENDING THE CHRISTIAN FAITH has always been challenging. Every age has its own particular obstacles and unique opportunities, and today is no different. At the outset we should be realistic about both the obstacles and the opportunities, for to do the work of apologetics with integrity we need to be clear about which hindrances are real and which may be imaginary.

One reason we are less than effective in doing apologetics today is rooted in the belief that our age is absolutely unique and that barriers to believing the gospel are far greater than ever before. According to this view, the Christian faith was more the consensus in earlier epochs. Compared to those days, we are in decline and secularization has gagged the message.

Different candidates for a golden age are put forth by different people. Some place it in the early church, when the gospel spread with astounding rapidity. Others look to the high Middle Ages, the era of the Gothic cathedral, when all of life and culture pointed to God. Protestants like to recall the Reformation or perhaps the Puritan days as times when the gospel had a great impact. A popular American version sees the colonial times as basically Christian. But we must ask honestly: Was the task of persuasion easier in the past than today? Were there times when the general cultural climate was more conducive to the gospel?

To be sure, extraordinary spiritual advances were made during certain periods of history, often despite great odds. Yet in order to avoid a wrong-minded nostalgia, we need a dose of historical honesty. Looking carefully beneath the surface of what is apparently an age of faith often reveals not only strengths but weaknesses.

In the early church, for example, there was indeed an extraordinary fervor as Christians faced not only philosophical opponents but also persecutors. At the same time, however, the church was full of dissension, skepticism, and corrupt practices. For example, Christians were slow to question the surrounding culture's views on privilege and thus it took a long time for the liberating message of the gospel to affect women and family life. Asceticism was often considered the most spiritual demeanor for true Christians. In the fourth century a confusion of power between the church and the state developed that is still being untangled today. Furthermore, Christian apologetics did not always clearly define the gospel over against Greek philosophy. Concepts were borrowed from philosophy that instead of making it understandable actually contradicted the gospel message.[1]

The same basic evaluation could be made of other candidates for a golden age. Medieval Europe represented a mixed civilization that knew great blessings. The influence of the gospel was behind advances in technology, hospice care, and the arts, but there were serious obstacles to faith as well. Because Christianity was the only official religion, it was difficult to distinguish between real faith and nominal practice. Many believed that grace was dispensed because one simply went to church or steered a child into the priesthood.

The same judgment holds true for colonial America, when the Puritans of Massachusetts Bay sought to bring all of life under the rule of God. The limited Christian consensus of Massachusetts, however, did not last very long. By the time of the Declaration of Independence and the Constitution, deism and other Enlightenment views were as influential as the Christian faith. At best there was a synthesis, a kind of "Christian humanism." And tragic flaws contradicted even the good face of humanism, such as the scandals of slavery and the treatment of Native Americans, which were not addressed seriously until much later—and then not altogether satisfactorily.

In short, doing effective apologetics was no easier in former times than today. There has never been a golden age when commending the faith was free from considerable obstacles.

NO GOLDEN PRESENT

Ironically, a number of people believe quite the opposite about the present—they hold that there has never been a better time to do effective apologetics than now. This conviction has many forms; we will briefly mention two.

The first form of optimism sees our era as a golden age of communication. The means whereby we communicate today are so powerful that people claim we have the best chance to spread the good news globally since the Reformation, which used the printing press to such advantage. Indeed, on the surface it appears that through television, popular books, radio, the Internet, and other media, the gospel could be made available to large populations with relative ease.

But the primary difficulty with this view is that it confuses means with ends. It does little good to have extensive communications networks if real persuasion is not occurring. The promise of communication is often ironically contradicted by the means of communication. For example, seeing a war battle on the televised news gives the viewer the sense of being there, of being on top of the situation. Watching the news on the television, however, actually makes us feel powerless to do anything about the war.

Christians can deceive themselves into thinking that modern methods will guarantee successful evangelism. One example is the multiplication of large conferences with thousands of Christians attending. There are meetings on evangelism, conferences on world missions, charismatic assemblies, and gatherings featuring a certain ministry or keynote speaker. From the sheer magnitude of these megaevents one has the impression that Christianity is a force to be reckoned with.

When examined closely, however, another side appears. Many in the audience travel from event to event, listening to inspiring speakers but rarely taking the message to the marketplace or the laboratory. The message itself is often familiar devotional language that does not touch the real world. For a brief moment, a mass of people experience a spiritual high that then vanishes.

This reinforces the tribalism that besets so many Christians today. No doubt it is involuntary tribalism—we long to have an influence on our world but do not know how. We fear the world because it is not responsive, and so we retreat to the safer haven of Christian fellowship.

Now we should be careful not to disparage the blessings of modern life. After all, who is not thankful for advances in medicine and for the relative prosperity and security of life in many parts of the West? Perhaps today all we have is a few "rainbows for the fallen world"[2]—but they are bright rainbows. Doing Christian apologetics is perhaps no easier today than in times past, but it is not necessarily harder.

POSTMODERN HOPE

The second form of optimism about the present says that our age is open as never before to the gospel because we are "postmodern." According to this view, one of the major obstacles to belief in the Christian faith is "modernity." This sweeping concept refers to the eighteenth-century Enlightenment movement that places all its trust in human reason and the inevitability of progress. Since that time, and up until World War II, there has been an embargo on the possibility of God.[3] But after the devastations of the war and the revolutions of the ensuing decades, the modern mentality has broken down. We can no longer believe in reason alone.

There is much that is appealing in the vision of the postmodern present as a great opportunity for the gospel.[4] Human reason as a rigid, universal standard is not finally compatible with a sovereign, creator God. But the end of the "Age of Reason" is not necessarily the beginning of the age of faith. For one thing, at the heart of the postmodern mentality is a culture of extreme skepticism. The postmodern *condition*, as French theorist François Lyotard calls it, is one in which what he calls the *grand narrative* (the "metanarrative") is ruled out.[5] There is no more truth; there is no more great key to the meaning of life. According to many postmodernists, knowledge is no longer objective—nor even useful—and ethics is not universal. All we have is data and language games. This is hardly a world compatible with the gospel.

Besides the problem that the Christian faith and the postmodern condition are not really compatible, there is a further difficulty with optimism about a golden present. The world after the World War II is not really so different from Enlightenment times as the postmodernists claim. It is not even certain that we have left modernity at all.

Sociologist Anthony Giddens has argued that when we understand its deepest structures, modernity is not so easily surpassed. Such basic features as trust in critical reason and faith in progress are still very much with us. Even disillusionment with reason, which is characteristic of trends after World War II, was there long before. Perhaps the most we could claim is that the criticism against the dominant traits of modernity is especially sharp today.[6]

In sum, there never was a golden age when evangelism was easier; today is no better, though no worse, than other times. To be sure, every era has different characteristics, needs, and challenges, and thus Christian apologetics must be alert to the peculiarities of an epoch. But the reason that today or any day represents a special opportunity—the reason that apologetics is *relevant*—is not primarily because we have a good understanding of the cultural context. Rather it is because of the message, the *good news* of the gospel. By definition it is fresh and even surprising. If "nothing is new under the sun" in human history, the message itself, coming from another world not ruled by the sun, is fresh in every way today.

BEYOND
CHEAP IMPACT

The dominant secularity exerts cognitive pressure
upon the religious consciousness. . . . Some people,
intellectuals as well as others, resolve this problem
by giving in to the pressures.
—Peter L. Berger, *The Heretical Imperative*, 1979

FALSE MOVES

DOING APOLOGETICS IN AN AUTHENTIC FASHION always involves
two concerns. One is that the message has integrity. The content
of the discourse must be faithful to the basic principles of the
Christian faith for it to make any true impact. The other is that
the message must be credible to those who hear it. We will have
to engage in what sociologist Peter Berger terms "bargaining"
with the modern world without giving in to its basic worldview.
In other words, we will have to "translate" the message into the
language of the day yet without capitulating to the pressure of the
secular mindset. This chapter is a brief exploration of some of
the dangers involved in the translation process. The medium
can compromise the message in at least three ways.

The first way we can compromise is when we lose patience
and attempt to gain a hearing by grasping for power, such as
through violence. All over the world today religious zealots are
trying to establish the kingdom of God by means of vigilante
justice. Seeking power can also be done in more subtle ways,

such as pressing for legislation or political change without altering the underlying spiritual factors that govern them.

This misunderstands the need for structures of *cultural authority*, a term that refers to the combination of religious and moral convictions that hold a society together. This is the "glue" that binds together each of the particular spheres of a given society, strengthening the whole. When we attempt to make an impact with the Christian faith but neglect the slow and patient work of bringing change to every sphere of society—the family, the workplace, the media, business, politics, and the rest—we are only dealing with the surface and real change eludes us. Frustrating as it may be to work at a deeper level over the long term, it is the only way to have a lasting impact for the gospel.

A second way of compromise moves in the opposite direction: Christian faith becomes "privatized," which means we are happy to hold to Christian beliefs but only for ourselves, not bothering anyone else with them. Privatization fits into a growing trend both in America and the West at large. According to sociologists, we are "going indoors," living life at home in front of the entertainment system or computer screen. We can do our banking without ever meeting a teller. We can discuss an issue over the Internet without facing our opponent.

Many Christians are satisfied to keep their faith for themselves without seeking to influence their neighbors. They are becoming a "tribal" people as they become increasingly isolated from the surrounding culture. This not only flies in the face of the clear biblical commandment not to hide our light under a bowl (Matthew 5:15), but also withholds from a needy society the benefits and healing power of the gospel.

Although this isolation appears to keep the Christian community free from the world, it actually breeds another kind of worldliness, one that creates its own safe haven from the turf God has placed us on. Although there is a place for contemplation and meditation in the Christian life, just as important is going out to the highways and meeting others. Christ's last commandment, after all, was to go out to all the nations and make disciples (Matthew 28:19).

A third misguided strategy, one that is closer to the ideal but still not in line with it, is what I would call "mere evangelism." With this approach people believe that because the world is a hostile environment—a place that will soon come to an end, being replaced by the new heavens and the new earth—they may preach a kind of one-dimensional salvation message. In effect, they look to save souls, not whole persons, aiming to get a large number into heaven.

In some ways, proclaiming the message of hope to a lost world does need the highest priority. But the biblical mandate is far broader than mere proclamation. After all, the commandment of Christ is to make disciples, not just to save souls. Proper evangelism is more balanced, appealing to the whole person; it has implications for the here and now, not merely for the world after.

The Apostle Paul, writing to the Romans, tells his readers over eleven densely written chapters about the wonders of the gospel of grace. Then in chapter 12, building on all that he said, he tells them how to live. The transition word is "therefore," and what follows is astonishing. One might have expected Paul the zealot, Paul who had persecuted the church but who now preaches the gospel, Paul the tireless missionary, to tell his readers, "Therefore go and seize power." Or, "Therefore just hold tight and pray." Or even, "Therefore get out there and win souls." He says none of these, but instead tells them to worship God with their bodies and their minds (12:1). In this way, they will be confirming how excellent God's will really is (12:2).

The will of God, in Paul's understanding, applies to all of life. He explains how in the ensuing chapters of his letter. The true worshipers will have a high regard for others and a low regard for themselves (12:3–13). They will obey authority, even when they are persecuted, and seek to live in peace with those around them (12:14–13:7); they will be concerned to live with ethical integrity (13:8–14); they will have special regard for less

mature Christians (14:1–15:6). This pattern displayed among
the Christians will make outsiders want to join (15:7–22).
Finally, along with Paul, followers of Christ will have a special
heart for the poor and the hungry (15:23–33).

The heart of Paul's argument is that only worship highlights
the ultimate purpose of the will of God because worship begins
where Christian living should, with the personal knowledge of
God himself. His person is his will; his character are his
commands.

In other words, though the three misguided strategies diminish the impact of the gospel, one strategy really promotes it: To
worship God, body and soul, heart and mind. When we are properly communing and conversing with the living God, we will
do a great deal of good on this earth. When we love God as we
should, we will love our neighbors as well. Part of loving our
neighbors is to commend the virtues of the gospel to them,
which is where apologetics comes in. To be heavenly minded is
not necessarily to be no earthly good. Paradoxically, those who
are most devoted to God are often the most productive in this
world.

TWO CITIES, TWO LOVES

Perhaps no better illustration of this paradox exists than the
apologetics of St. Augustine (354–430). Bishop of Hippo in
North Africa, Augustine lived at a time when the Roman
Empire was in sharp decline. Citizens were looking for a scape-
goat and blamed the Christians for the deterioration of the
Empire. When the "Eternal City" was sacked by the Goths in
410 A.D., the church was said to be the cause; because Christians believed in only one God, it was argued, the church was
corrupting the City. The pagan gods of Rome were older and
could be trusted to protect the people from its enemies, but the
Christian faith intruded by declaring that there is only one God.
Because this "new" religion accepted no synthesis with other
religions and its God refused to belong to the Roman pantheon

of Gods, the pagan gods no longer protected the City. Rome's downfall was thus blamed on the uncooperative believers in an uncooperative God.

Augustine's answer to this attack was his extraordinary treatise against paganism, *The City of God*. In it he argues that whether one begins with Greek philosophy, Roman life, or biblical prophecy, there can only be one truth because only one God fits the aspirations of all people. Continuing, he says that the church is not at fault for Rome's troubles, and Rome would be a better place—far better than the gods could create—if this single truth were confessed.

Against the charge of disloyalty, Augustine states that the hope of heaven actually makes life on this earth more productive, not less. Far from being uncooperative, Christians are better citizens, more generous to the poor and greater peace-makers, than the pagans. The parallels between the fifth century and our own are obvious.

The charge is often made today that the world is in trouble because of widespread intolerance. Religious people are especially intolerant because they believe in one truth, it is said. Sadly, as we have seen, there are fanatics who do embrace wrong-headed strategies. But if we follow Paul's discussion in Romans 12, we should reach a very different outlook. Love for the "City of God" means more involvement, not less, with the "City of Man." The worship of God means a better apologetic, not a weaker one.

We could use apologetic answers like Augustine's in our own day. His approach was two-fold, being negative in the sense that he dismantled the case against the church with careful scholarly investigation of the facts. But more fundamentally it was positive: Augustine answered the charges made against the gospel by constructing a Christian worldview.

The City of God was nothing less than the beginnings of a new philosophy of history. Instead of the ancients' cyclical view it puts forth a linear approach in which history is moving from a beginning to an end. However complex and contradictory the various trends, history is relentlessly moving toward the grand climax when God will judge the world and establish a new order. This apologetic, in other words, is global and all-encompassing.

When we rightly understand both the obstacles and the opportunities of our world we can be both realistic and hopeful—realism with hope, or better, realism *because* of hope. Thus the impact we make will be deeply authentic.

3

APOSTOLIC APOLOGY

The Christian faith rests not merely upon great teachings or philosophies, not upon the charisma of a leader, not upon the success of raising moral values, not upon the skill or eloquence or good works of its advocates. . . . Christianity rests on historic truth.

—Charles Colson, *Loving God*, 1983

LESSONS FROM FIRST PETER

IN BASING A CONCEPT SUCH AS APOLOGETICS on the Bible we need to recognize that there will not necessarily exist one proof-text, let alone a Hebrew or Greek word to justify that concept. Similarly, the concept of *sacrament* is not based on a verse or term in the original languages but rather on a biblical theme taken from its general teaching. As it happens in the case of apologetics, however, a most significant verse in the New Testament carries a good deal of weight. Thus we will begin with the verse and then move to the large biblical horizon.

The key verse is 1 Peter 3:15, which says, "But in your hearts set apart Christ as Lord. Always be prepared to give an answer [*apologia*] to everyone who asks you to give the reason for the hope that you have. But do this with gentleness and respect. . . ." The Greek term *apologia* is a noun that literally means "apology"; the verb *apologeomai* means to give a defense. These terms occur eighteen times in the New Testament, and various Hebrew equivalents can be found throughout the Old Testament.

All but a few of the references have judicial, courtroom connotations. For example, our Lord told his disciples, "When you are brought before synagogues, rulers and authorities, do not worry about how you will *defend* yourselves or what you will say" (Luke 12:11, my emphasis). Or, again, the Apostle Paul often went before such rulers as Felix, Festus, and Agrippa to set forth a case in *defense* of his position.[1]

The letter is first of all one of encouragement.[2] From various expressions used, we know that the readers were in adversity. Peter refers to them as "exiles of the dispersion" (1:1, NRSV) and says, "I have written to you briefly, encouraging you and testifying that this is the true grace of God. *Stand fast* in it" (5:12, my emphasis). The central message of the letter has been aptly expressed by theologian Edmund P. Clowney: "Facing impending assaults on the gospel, Peter witnesses to the grace of God, the overwhelming reality of what God has done in Jesus Christ."[3] Going further, we can see within this central message there is a particular concern with the Christian response to *suffering*.

Our passage about apologetics is certainly concerned with suffering, as a look at the context reveals. Beginning with verses 13–14 of the third chapter, we learn Peter's philosophy—that everyone, including followers of Christ, must suffer in this life. Often we are surprised by suffering, feeling guilty and wondering what is wrong, yet no simple cause may exist.

But the suffering of Christians has a purpose. Although it may not be possible to identify the immediate cause, in the larger context of God's purposes, there is meaning to our experience. The great Old Testament figure Job did not know and never really found out why he had to face such affliction in his life. Yet we see in the account that there certainly was a purpose in his case.

Ultimately, according to Peter's outlook, not only does suffering have a purpose, but no final harm can come to Christians. "You are blessed," he says. Not because suffering leads to improvement, but because in suffering we have fellowship with Christ. Those who have experienced it recognize this mystery.

And so, we need not have fear (verse 14); no terror that somehow we will be disarmed. In Jesus' words already mentioned, fear is also in the outlook: *fear not* when they drag you up, *fear not* what you shall say in your defense (*apologeomai* is the verb).[4] These words to the disciples must have made quite an impression on Peter. When there is a proper defense, fear is not needed.

In verse 15 he continues, "but in your hearts set apart [sanctify, reverence] Christ as Lord." Here the apostle makes a kind of equation or a trade-off: As we lift up Christ, we lose fear. This spiritual principle has a psychological dimension in that when we focus on Christ, other thoughts "grow strangely dim."

Far more important, however, is the fact that this principle depends on objective truth. Because God has overcome evil, as we look to the Lord we realize nothing else can threaten our position. Indeed nothing else compares to his victory: "If God is for us, who can be against us?" (Romans 8:31) Peter knew about this comparison, for in that dreadful night when Christ was captured he lost nerve, forgetting to lift God up (Matthew 26:69–74). By the time he wrote this letter, however, he had been forgiven and restored, and held a key position in the early church that required great courage.

Peter in his letter is actually adapting Isaiah 8:12–13, which is a warning to the Israelites not to follow the ways of the Assyrians, their greatest threat.[5] The people of God were continually tempted to trust in powerful nations rather than in the LORD. Isaiah, however, calls them not to "fear what [the Assyrians] fear," but to fear the LORD. They are to "set him apart," being devoted to God as Savior and transcendent LORD.[6]

FROM FEAR TO FAITH

Here then is the Old Testament confirmation of our great spiritual principle: As we fear God, other fears diminish. Most of us know that the "fear of the Lord" in the Old Testament does not mean terror but rather confident awe before a God who is both powerful and good. A little episode in C. S. Lewis's *Chronicles of Narnia* illustrates this well. Lucy asks whether Aslan, the great lion who represents Christ in the story, is quite safe. She hears, "No, Lucy, Aslan is not safe, but he is good."

Confidence in God's goodness enables us to say with Isaiah, "do not call conspiracy all that they call conspiracy." Living in a hostile world, we may think of many threats—some are imaginary, many are real. Apologetics recognizes the reality of opposition, but gives answers in the confidence that God's goodness is ultimate.

The opposition Christians faced in the first century was rooted in many sources, such as physical persecution, verbal assaults, or more subtle means. Verse 15 in 1 Peter 3 is surely about verbal hostility, as we see not only from the clause, "to everyone who asks you," but from the context. Peter is discussing the kinds of suffering that one may experience, such as persecution with "questions" of an accusatory nature intended to provoke a reaction.

Peter tells the readers to be on guard, to be gentle, to keep a clear conscience. Indeed most apologetics discussions are far more than intellectual games. Issues of truth, life, and meaning rarely evoke indifference when raised by seekers and skeptics. We are doing spiritual battle when we do apologetics.

Following Peter's reasoning, we see that the most important weapon for this spiritual contest is straightening out our own state of being. As he terms it, the basic issues occur in the human heart, which in the biblical understanding is the center of a person. Here is where the issues of life are determined.[7] The heart is our center, our first priority, because it is the place where our basic commitments are held; thus the Proverbs tell us to "guard the heart above all things" (Proverbs 4:20–23).

Peter then moves the discussion to a New Testament reality, adapting the Isaiah passage to its fulfillment in Christ: "Reverence *Christ* as Lord." Quoting Isaiah but changing the terms slightly, he says in effect, "sanctify the Lord, the Christ." Again, in Clowney's words: "[Peter] is explicitly identifying the One who slept in the stern of the fishing boat with the almighty Creator of heaven and earth."[8]

This is what Jesus taught in his final discourse to the apostles before he left this world, as recorded in John 14–16. He said that there will be tribulation or fear in this world. But if we recognize and trust Christ, if we "see him," as, say, Philip had difficulty doing during that discourse, we lose the fear of the world.[9]

KNOWING THE ANSWERS

Moving on with Peter's argument, we understand that as we set Christ apart and lose our fear of the world we begin to be ready. He tells the reader always to be prepared to do apologetics. Put simply, readiness involves two things: knowledge of the answers and sensitivity to the needs. First, then, what message should we tell those who ask hard questions? Peter's answer is interesting—the word *hope* is one of his favorite ways to describe the Christian message.[10]

In the Bible the word hope does not carry the connotation of uncertainty that our modern usage has. When we say, "I hope the war ends soon," or "I do hope I hear from my friend," there is the real possibility of another outcome from the desired one. But in New Testament usage, the word has a quite different ring, meaning such confidence about the outcome that we are willing to stake everything on it. The gospel does not deal in wishes but in an utter certainty: "I know whom I have believed," says Paul. This is because, according to him, there is, "Christ in you, the *hope* of glory" (Colossians 1:27). Our Christian hope is our sure knowledge that the message is true; it is hope that "does not disappoint us" (Romans 5:5).[11] As the writer of Hebrews puts it, "Let us hold unswervingly to the hope we profess, for he who promised is faithful (Hebrews 10:23).

This wonderful message, however appropriate to explain the present, is also and essentially a promise of things to come, based on the utterly sure thing that Christ died for sinners and was raised according to the Scriptures. This hope is the coming of the kingdom, the conquest of Jesus and his love over the world and all areas of our lives. As the great Dutch statesman and theologian Abraham Kuyper was fond of saying, "There is not one square inch of the entire creation about which Jesus Christ does not cry out, 'This is mine! This belongs to me!' "[12] If the Christian faith is true, then this is not arrogance nor the insecure claims of a bombast or fanatic, but a message of liberty, grace, and hope.

Notice in our key verse that the work of apologetics is verbal. If apologetics has a prominent legal sense and means "getting oneself off a charge," we see that verbal defense is especially in view. This needs to be stressed in light of the sincere but misguided idea that somehow putting things in words destroys the authenticity of God's truth. Even the great Charles Spurgeon was fond of saying that defense of the gospel was "sheer impertinence." He maintained that apologetics was something akin to defending a lion, and that it is better simply to let him out of his cage: "Never mind defending Deuteronomy or the whole of the Pentateuch. Preach Jesus Christ and him crucified."[13]

This is a powerful objection in that we should be reluctant to do anything that undermines or contradicts the power of the gospel. Thus, much the way a literary critic might ruin a good poem, some people feel it is an affront to interfere with the gospel by a human defense of any sort. But the flaw here is twofold. First, those who argue like that ignore the fact that the gospel never stands alone; it always requires some kind of agency to bring it within earshot of real people. Second, we miss the wonder of the way God actually chooses to work. No doubt he could have arranged to proclaim the truth himself with no human persuasive skills. But instead he gives us the great honor of using our weak, fragile human agency to carry the precious treasure of the divine message.

Acts 10 contains a revealing episode exemplifying how God works through people. While the God-fearing (Gentile) Cornelius was at prayer, an angel appeared to him and announced that his prayers were answered. He would need to receive a man called Peter and hear his message. In the meantime, Peter was receiving a vision in which he was being told to accept all food, even previously forbidden food, as clean. It was a prelude to opening the gospel to the Gentiles. Peter then went to Cornelius's house, preached the message of hope, and Cornelius and his family received God's grace.

The astonishing thing in the account is that while the angel was speaking to Cornelius he might as well have proclaimed the gospel message. For one thing, it would have saved a lot of time and effort. But he didn't. Further, the voice that addressed Peter might as well have spoken to Cornelius. Instead, the Lord chose to involve human agency in the preaching of the gospel, and so it has been ever since. Those who avoid doing apologetics in the name of "letting the Lord do his own work" end up appearing more spiritual than God himself.

KNOWING THE NEEDS

The second part of the readiness commended by Peter is also instructive. It is not enough to have great answers if we do not recognize the need and understand our audience. Part of the skills required for apologetics is to know a bit of psychology. Those of us who remember watching Francis Schaeffer of l'Abri, the little Swiss mountain community, answer questions recall his almost uncanny sense of detecting the "problem behind the problem" in many students.

But another, more crucial, part of recognizing the need involves understanding the times, which is as much a matter of spiritual wisdom as scientific ability to monitor trends and cultural currents. A brief but telling account of the tribe of Issachar in 1 Chronicles 12:32 models the kind of perception Peter asks for: "men who *understood* the times and knew what Israel should do." This gift of understanding gave Issachar the ability to assess the culture of the people surrounding Israel and then counsel rulers such as David.

Similarly, Jesus alluded to the need for such wisdom. He rebuked the Scribes for recognizing the signs of the weather but missing the historic moment being played out before them.[14] To cite Spurgeon again, but favorably this time: he recommended that Christians hold a Bible in one hand and a newspaper in the other, comparing them constantly. Readers who are familiar with the depth and quality of certain European newspapers will understand the full import of Spurgeon's recommendation.

The conscientious reader may not feel competent to evaluate trends and judge the drift of the surrounding culture, wondering if it is possible to do apologetics without being current with all that is going on. The answer is two-fold. First, every Christian has a specific call from the Lord. Not all are asked to do up-front cutting-edge cultural apologetics. Some will be effective simply sharing their wisdom or giving their testimony. Others will not say much, but when they do, they will be noticed for their integrity. Peter does not say, "Know all the answers"; he says, "Be prepared."

The second answer is that each Christian ought to take an interest in some areas of human psychology and social analysis. This may mean serious investigation, such as taking courses and reading texts; or discussing books and trends in a fellowship group; or developing a certain sense of life's character without formal training. Whatever one's calling, in order to follow Peter's mandate some hard work is ahead.

But one final word: The basic way to be prepared is not described as primarily intellectual. The beginning of 1 Peter 3:15 says, "in your hearts set apart Christ as Lord . . . [b]ut do this with gentleness and respect, keeping a clear conscience." In other words, not only must we have the right words, we need to speak in the right way. We probably know people who can win every argument but lose the person in front of them or even their own soul, since their lives may not exhibit what they claim. None of us lives anywhere close to perfection, but to an apologist a sound spiritual life is never a luxury.

Apologetics, then, is about *argument*, which means developing a persuasive sequence of words to answer the challenges from an unbelieving culture. There is thus an affinity, but not direct similarity, between apologetics and evangelism. Evangelism is a missionary endeavor, proclaiming the gospel in every circumstance. Apologetics is a part of this missionary thrust, specializing in argument as it focuses on issues and methods that "demolish arguments and every pretension that sets itself up against the knowledge of God" (2 Corinthians 10:5). So apologetics is a kind of science, a discipline that develops sound ways of presenting the gospel.

THE LARGER BIBLICAL MANDATE

"Come now, let us reason together," says the LORD.
—Isaiah, eighth century B.C.

ROOTS IN THE OLD TESTAMENT

TO JUSTIFY THE WORK OF APOLOGETICS biblically the classical text from Peter would be mandate enough. But we can go much further. If we accept the preliminary definition of apologetics as sound argument, we see all of Scripture testifying to the need for apologetics.

Just as the Bible does not begin with the gospels, let alone the epistles, nor does the work of apologetics stem only from the New Testament. The Old Testament background for persuasive argument is strong and rich. From the very beginning the battleground for truth was "apologetic"; Satan's temptation of Eve was based on a (faulty) argument about authority and wisdom. The very failure of the first couple to respond properly is answered by God's grace in the form of an apologetic argument. The LORD God first presents the argument against the serpent in what is sometimes called the "first gospel" (Genesis 3:14–15) with its powerful apologetic message to humanity, culminating in the promise, "he will crush your head, and you will strike his heel." The ultimate outcome of history is the downfall of evil and the victory of the authentic Seed, Christ himself. Then an argument is presented against the woman and the man, telling them how they would live with all of human posterity under the regime of a fallen world.

From then on in the Old Testament the truth is argued for by various people in various different ways—from Noah, who preached to his generation about judgment, to Qoheleth (the author of Ecclesiastes), who shows the futility of life without God, to David, who argues that truth will eventually triumph against what appears to be prevailing now (Psalm 37).

The prophets are especially instructive for doing apologetics. Isaiah, for example, carries on a strong appeal for truth. The LORD through him pleads with the people of Israel, "Come now, let us reason together,"[1] and he challenges the idolaters to "present their case" (41:21). "Set forth your arguments," he says, telling them with considerable irony to use some counter-apologetics. In short, he is asking for a courtroom debate where the truth will be tested.

Prophetic apologetics can be negative, as found in Ezekiel 14:1–4. Here God responds to idolaters who wish to inquire of the prophet, saying he will *answer* himself and recapture their hearts.[2] Notice the idea is very much one of arguing persuasively against another position. But it can also be positive, as in Jeremiah 15:19–21 where the LORD says, "If you repent, I will restore you that you may serve me; if you utter *worthy*, not *worthless*, words, you will be my spokesman. Let this people turn to you, but you must not turn to them. . . ."[3]

We have here a kind of apologetic about-face. Theologically speaking, sin entails guilt. God, the just accuser, has a case against us; because of his grace, however, the case actually turns in our favor when he himself pleads it. If only we would turn to him, God would actually accuse our accuser and terminate our guilt through the work of Christ.[4]

One more facet of the about-face can be mentioned. Not only does God accuse the accuser, but he does so by becoming the sinner's substitute, putting himself on trial so that believers would not have to be condemned. When the Israelites were wandering in the desert and accused Moses of having led them into a land of no water, God's remedy is astounding. He tells Moses to beat down with his rod of judgment on the rock where God himself stood. In other words, Moses was to judge God instead of the people. Water poured out of the rock—the water of life—foretelling Jesus' life-giving sacrifice on the cross (Exodus 17:1–7). Apologetics is possible because God has made a successful case against sin and guilt, which were born by his own Son.

APOLOGETICS AND WISDOM

The Bible's wisdom literature is a particularly rich source of apologetic material. Basically, wisdom refers to the ability to think through and live out the mysteries of human existence. Its beginning point is the fear of the Lord,[5] but its end is in all of human experience. Wisdom literature consists of several types, such as the short, pregnant sayings in Proverbs that prescribe rules for living well and condemn folly, or a meditation on the enigmas of life as found in the book of Job. This genre is also evident in Ecclesiastes, the Sermon on the Mount, portions of the letter of James, and various parts of Paul's epistles.

The book of Job is an extraordinary statement on the problem of God's justice, an exploration of why a believer may be afflicted. Indeed, Job's righteousness was not so much that he was good, but that he was faithful. It is this believing person who is severely tested, and the source of his testing is Satan's direct challenge to God.

The drama of the story unfolds on several levels. First, a major ethical issue is presented and eventually resolved. If people are afflicted, does it mean that they have sinned and deserve it? Behind this idea lies a more basic view of the nature of God: Is God not simply the rewarder of justice and the punisher of guilt? Job's friends try to convince him of this, making a simplistic connection between suffering and personal guilt. In the end, however, Job is vindicated and the friends are shown to have narrowly categorized sin, punishment, and God's way of enforcing the law.

Second, Job grows during this process. In the beginning he is a righteous man with child-like faith; when the horrendous trials come he enters a new stage of his life, a sort of adolescence when doubt and agony crowd in on his former security. Though he never denies God, he questions him, sometimes appropriately, sometimes not. In his dialogues with his friends he is capable of strong affirmations of wisdom: "I know that my Redeemer lives, and in the end he will stand upon the earth" (Job 19:25). But he also comes close to attributing evil motives to God himself: "You turn on me ruthlessly. . . . Surely no one lays a hand on a broken man when he cries for help in his distress" (30:21, 24); he nears the arrogance he denounces in his friends: "I sign now my defense—let the Almighty answer me" (31:35).

Finally, however, Job moves from spiritual adolescence to the mature sage after God finally does speak to him, but most severely, reminding him of his finitude and folly (chapters 38–41). Job is utterly humbled: "Therefore I despise myself and repent in dust and ashes" (42:6); he is also rewarded for his great faithfulness despite the errors of his adolescence.

The third issue in this apologetic piece is the vindication of God's plan. Neither is the LORD simply the divine supervisor of abstract law nor dissolved by Job's pleas; instead he is the one who overcomes both Satan[6] and the curse of the law. His plan involves salvation through the covenant. The Old Testament people of God form the necessary link from the promise of Genesis 3:15 to Jesus Christ: Job had a part in the history of redemption as a figure of Christ.

As we know from the New Testament, God's plan comes down to salvation by grace based on the work of Christ through faith. Real faith shows its authenticity by the way we live and speak. Had Job failed—had his life or speech shown that his faith was not authentic—the plan would have demonstrably not been valid. God would have been shown to be a liar and evil would have had its way.

This is the ultimate issue: Does God know whether the plan of salvation can work? Is the obedience of Christ effective; is faith enough? The overwhelming answer in this extraordinary argument from wisdom literature is affirmative.

We should also note that the New Testament presents no less a case for wisdom than the Old. Jesus often spoke in the wisdom tradition, couching his speeches in the language of parable or proverb. Portions of the letters of the apostles are cast in a wisdom vein. And the book of James, too, is a New Testament wisdom epistle, brilliantly reminding believers of the need to cultivate humility and patience when faced with the obvious injustices of life. Like its counterpart, Ecclesiastes, James argues that appearances are misleading—the rich seem to have it over the poor, the smart-tongued over the simple. But in the end what matters is following the "royal law found in Scripture" (2:8). Thus through wisdom in the New Testament the art of persuasion that leads to belief is set forth marvelously.

CONFIRMATION IN THE NEW TESTAMENT

There is a well-known maxim about the relationship of the Old and New Testaments: "The New is in the Old concealed, the Old is in the New revealed." What is contained in the Old Testament in seed form comes to full fruition in the New Testament; the theme of apologetics is no exception. We do not have to go far into the gospels to realize that at their core they set forth a case for the Christian faith. Matthew begins with a genealogy of Christ to prove to his Jewish readers that Jesus is truly the promised child of Israel's fathers, including Abraham and David. Luke, the scientist, begins his account by asserting that what he has written is the result of solid historical research. John, whose gospel is quite different from the first three, tells his readers that his purpose is to record conversations and events in order that they might believe and thus have life in Christ's name (John 20:31).

As we read the gospels we learn a great deal about the way apologetics is central to Christ's mission. From one angle, much of Jesus' ministry is couched in terms of apologetics. In fact, the pattern of opposition to him, culminating in his condemnation to the cross, becomes a kind of pattern for Christians who experience the same basic types of opposition.

There is a remarkable but rarely noticed episode about Jesus as an apologist in Luke. Simeon's prophecy over the infant Savior announced the prominence of a key aspect of Christ's life that relates directly to argument and self-vindication because of the opposition against him. Simeon, looking at the infant, said, "This child is destined to cause the falling and rising of many in Israel, and to be a sign that will be spoken against, so that the thoughts of many hearts will be revealed. . ." (Luke 2:34–35).

Here we see the heart of apologetics. Naturally, Jesus' work is unique, and we are not to be would-be messiahs. But at the same time we participate in the work of his kingdom, seeking to be Christ-like in all circumstances. And as our Lord told us, when people speak against us as believers it is fundamentally against him that they speak (John 15:18–27). Apologetics is our response on behalf of Christ, for the sake of Christ.

Moving beyond the gospels and into the rest of the New Testament, we note that this pattern of responding for Christ and because of Christ is certainly the apostolic pattern. Think of Paul, who was often dragged up before the authorities. Opposition to the gospel is not just a matter of misunderstanding, nor that unbelievers formulate their reluctance in a legitimized fashion. God surely permits a process by which error and hostility emerge when the truth is proclaimed. When Paul wrote to the Corinthians about his plans, for example, he said, "But I will stay on at Ephesus until Pentecost, because a great door for effective work has opened to me, and there are many who oppose me."[7]

Here, then, is a clear New Testament call, as rooted in the Old, to have sound apologetics and Christian argument. We should understand as well that when we argue faithfully for the truth of the message, we are not doing it alone or in our own clever rhetorical power. To the Thessalonians Paul says that the gospel came "with the Holy Spirit and with *deep conviction*."[8]

Notice no incompatibility in Paul's mind between the Spirit and persuasion;[9] indeed the Holy Spirit must do the invisible work in the heart. The Spirit uses our words and our arguments, but they are empty if he is not working with them and through them.

The work of apologetics fits in to the larger scheme of God's plan of redemption and is for all disciples; it is not a luxury for a few academics or specialists. This calling is part and parcel of bringing humanity back to God. Again, the apostle Paul brings this out in a marvelous passage about reconciliation (2 Corinthians 5:11–6:2) in which he tells the readers that God is busy reconciling the world to himself, forgiving sin and giving new life in Christ (5:19). Paul is a particularly persuasive ambassador for Christ, for he is driven by the same love that motivated Christ to heal the nations (5:14). In that compelling love, he brings the message of reconciliation to those who need to hear it. In other words, Paul's allegiance to God and his love enables him to do Christian apologetics. Thus he says, "Since, then, we know what it is to fear the Lord, we try to persuade men" (5:11).[10] Notice that this is virtually the same discussion of the two kinds of fear stressed in the text from 1 Peter 3:15—reverence for Christ and fear of hostile confrontation.

The work of doing apologetics is not simply a defensive response to attack, for there is also an "offensive" aspect to the warfare. To be sure, the weapons of this warfare are not worldly, but spiritual. Further on in 2 Corinthians Paul says, "We demolish arguments and every pretension that sets itself up against the knowledge of God, and we take captive every thought to make it obedient to Christ" (10:5). Many Christians have the uneasy feeling that there is something indecent about strong words. But speaking the truth forcefully is not necessarily unkind; in fact, it can be the kindest behavior toward another human being who does not know the truth.

Thus apologetics in the Bible, both in the Old and the New Testaments, is deeply involved in the overall design of the divine purpose. Only when we see the connection between the love of God and the work of persuasion will we feel at home doing apologetics. Only when we see how God's plan of salvation uses fragile, finite human beings as his heralds will we be compelled to argue for the faith despite our weaknesses. Why do we explore and defend the reasons of the heart? Because of the love of God. This, then, is apologetics from a biblical point of view: "Since, then, we know what it is to fear the Lord, we try to persuade men" (2 Corinthians 5:11).

5

A RICH PALETTE

> Only when men have nothing to hide from
> themselves and from their counterparts in the
> discussion will the way be opened for a dialogue
> that seeks to convince rather than to repel.
> —Herman Dooyeweerd,
> *Roots of Western Culture*, 1975

You Know It's True

AFTER LAYING THE BIBLICAL FOUNDATION for the task of apologetics, we now will discuss method. At the outset we need to underline that there are many valid arguments and various effective ways to persuade. In fact, most of us would be repelled or offended by a strict demonstration that moved from point A to point B and C and then claimed to have arrived at the final proof in point D. Rather than setting forth a method in this sense, we will outline an approach that banks on four realities. Because these truths are not steps in a chain but verities drawn from a rich palette, they may be used in any variety of ways.

The first issue is an ancient preoccupation in apologetics, matching the message to the audience or making a "point of contact." Over the centuries people have debated about where that point of contact is. Is it because people are reasonable and so we can communicate when we properly use reason? From Pascal's phrase, reasons of the heart, we realize that unaided, unqualified reason is not enough; people are more than rational machines. Besides, our rationality is tainted by our motives, sin, and self-interest.

A famous story told by a nineteenth-century philosopher shows why reason alone will not work as a point of contact. A man came into his doctor's office and declared that he was dead. The doctor tried to understand, saying, "Of course, we will all die." The patient replied, "No. I mean I am now actually dead." After more discussion the doctor finally did an experiment, asking his patient if he agreed that dead men don't bleed. The patient agreed. The doctor then pricked him with a needle to see if blood would come out; it did. "I guess I was wrong," exclaimed the patient, "dead men do bleed!"

If the point of contact does not lie in unaided reason, where is it? Simply put, the Bible sees it in the knowledge everyone already possesses of God's reality. According to Romans 1:19–21 all people know God, being surrounded by his revelation. Whether or not they fully acknowledge him or process the information correctly, every person is aware of God just by virtue of being human.

The great reformer John Calvin argued that each person is endowed with a "seed of religion." He said, "There is within the human mind, and indeed by natural instinct, an awareness of divinity" that is placed there by God, who "repeatedly shed[s] fresh drops."[1] The awareness of divinity of which Calvin speaks extends to rationality and morals. Human beings are not simply "religious, strangely imbued with a capacity for spirituality," as it is said today. We are actually God-conscious. Not only knowledge but moral sense is possible because we know God already.

This point is no doubt controversial. The Bible states it baldly without any explanation, yet the knowledge of God is not readily apparent in many unbelievers—because of a complicating factor. Though it is perfectly true that human beings *have* God's revelation, it does not follow that they *process* it correctly. Again, according to Romans 1, though we know God, we refuse to acknowledge him or give him thanks. What Paul literally says is that we suppress the truth, "holding" it in unrighteousness. The Greek word means something like "put into prison." That is, in refusing to be thankful to the Creator, we put the truth behind bars.

Thus in effect, Paul says that in various ways and through various expressions, all people are somehow hiding from the God they really know. We live in a kind of contradiction, a paradox: On the one hand everyone has a religious impulse, whether overtly religious or not. Yet on the other hand, somewhere that impulse has gone wrong.

This paradox has many forms. Some people are strongly convinced of God's presence but reject his requirements. Others have high ethical standards but cannot see why God is needed to justify them. But what matters is that the deep-rooted knowledge of God all people have is closely connected with morality, personal relations, guilt, aesthetics, and so on—in short, with all that counts in our experience. The conflict between what we know deep down and what we construct as a substitute for or escape from God will naturally be revealed in various ways. Thus one person may have terrible guilt from rejecting her childhood faith; another may be frustrated in a search for unrequited artistic fulfillment; and yet another may be obsessed with achievement in the business world but gradually realize how unhappy he is. These are all cases of religious conflict because they are connected with God's presence and requirements.

Religion is in one way quite uniform, being derived from a sense of dependence on something or someone that has ultimate value. Much religion, however, has gone wrong. Instead of trusting the true God, people turn to other objects of devotion. Though extremely varied throughout the world, at heart is a universal dynamic, the paradox of knowing and yet imprisoning the truth. In other words, the essence of religion is neither ritual nor creedal formulation nor ethical code but "faith."

Some argue that Western society has in fact abandoned religion altogether, becoming secular. But according to Paul's argument, although formal or institutional religion may be threatened in the West, a state of affairs without religion altogether is impossible. Despite current appearances of secularity, we can witness the strong presence of the religious drive gone wrong in at least two ways. First, as sociologist Jacques Ellul and others have pointed out, instead of the older faith of Christendom we now have faith in modernity.[2] Our religious confidence has been transferred from trust in God to newer god substitutes, such as science and technology, nation-building, hedonistic pleasure, and so on.[3]

Second, perhaps in reaction to the emptiness of the graceless modern world, many new religious movements have emerged. Some are closely tied to mainstream Christianity but have a special emphasis on experience and ministry. Others range from groups influenced by the East to New Age gnosticism, Psychic Friends, and the like.

Avoiding religion is thus impossible. This being so, when we attempt to argue for the Christian faith with unbelievers we are not talking to those for whom God's existence is strange or exotic. When we come to people with the claims of the truth, we are appealing to what they know but deny. We are asking them to be like the prodigal son and come to themselves. Again, Romans spells this out clearly: "[S]ince what may be known about God is plain to them, because God has made it plain to them" (1:19). The reason we may hold people accountable to God is that although they deny him, they know he is there: "For although they knew God, they neither glorified him as God nor gave thanks to him" (1:21).[4] This point carries an implication that is critical for apologetics: We have an assured point of contact with all human beings.

THE BELIEF BEHIND THE BELIEF

From this biblical assessment of the human condition it follows that some apologetic strategies are better than others. But which method of persuasion both counts on the knowledge of God people already possess and yet realizes they are walking away from him?

The best apologetics is not a series of dry methods, but is rather a wise discernment ensuring the kind of flexibility appropriate to working with a person's multidimensional spiritual life. The second apologetic reality, following on the point of contact, is what we will call disclosure. In essence this means moving onto the ground of an unbelieving person in order to uncover the inner dynamics of his or her worldview. The purpose is to help the person see how that position cannot provide the crucial answers for the human predicament. Strategies that seek to unmask the inner dynamics of someone's belief system may range from direct confrontation to gentle appeal, depending on the kind of resistance to the gospel that our interlocutor may have.

Years ago at l'Abri a remarkable visitor came to challenge biblical belief. Helen was an articulate and passionate skeptic whose main quarrel with the Christian faith was that it was founded on the idea of Christ's sacrifice. What she found objectionable was her perceived notion of the callous treatment of animals in the Old Testament. A fervent anti-vivisectionist, Helen's passionate cause was the protection of animal life.

In an extended conversation with Francis Schaeffer a kind of jousting match developed. Although he acknowledged that there was unnecessary cruelty to animals, especially in laboratories, he argued that animals could be used legitimately to serve various human needs. Helen could not agree, and countered that the God of the Old Testament was heartless and brutal because he authorized the sacrifice of goats and lambs.

After going around in circles for a while, Schaeffer suddenly looked down at Helen's feet. He pointed to her shoes, and asked why she was wearing leather! This was not meant to be a trick, but a way to show this skeptic that however committed she was to her position, it did not square with reality. From that point Helen was far less aggressive, and Schaeffer was able to speak more freely of the reasons for animal sacrifice. Discussing the sin that was symbolized by the sacrifice of Christ, he showed why the brutality of the cross was the only remedy for the human condition.

Disclosure may occur unexpectedly. Years ago I was a school teacher, and as one of the few Christians on the staff I often had discussions about the claims of the gospel with my colleagues. Bruce was a chemistry teacher with a strong dose of skepticism. We often met in the smoke-filled faculty room and vigorously discussed everything from ethics to the nature of the universe. He was convinced that no other explanation was needed for the intricacies of the material world except chance, and that religion was not only unnecessary but generally harmful. Our discussions forced me to be as cogent as possible, for Bruce was an engaging and remarkably honest person.

One day Bruce came into the faculty room with a strange expression on his face, walked right over to me, and said we needed to talk. I dropped what I was working on and listened intently as he described a chemistry experiment he had just conducted. I doubt I fully understood it at the time, but I clearly remember his avowal. "Bill," he said, "I am not prepared to admit that you have been right all along, but I simply have to confess that what I saw today in my laboratory was extraordinary and beautiful. How could such a thing occur only by chance? Maybe there is a designer after all. . . ." From that moment on, our conversations took on a very different tone.

If the Christian faith is true, then however consistently an unbeliever may appear to be living out his or her position, it cannot hold together. Somewhere there is a flaw, because we do in fact live in God's world. It may be a flaw of logic, emotion, or simply the irony of unsuccessful pride. The work of the apologist is to uncover the tension between unbelief and the knowledge of God that everyone has.

With a certain kind of skeptic, disclosure is often achieved when we can show that no one is without religion. Christians frequently find ourselves described as "religious," as though we had an irrational commitment to something unprovable. The assumption behind the allegation is that skeptics are free from such irrational faith. At this point the apologist needs to show that skepticism rests on a faith commitment that actually has less grounding than theism. Once an unbeliever acknowledges the universal role of faith it is much easier to move on to discussions of the validity of the gospel.

Coming Home

This brings us to the third methodological reality, what we will call homecoming, which must ride in tandem with the second. We fail in our apologetics if we stop with the unmasking of unbelief, even though it may be easier to diagnose than to cure. Such an emphasis, however, is not only unbiblical but cruel, because it leaves people in a hopeless position. In 1 Peter 3:15 we saw that the primary responsibility of the believer is to present the reasons for hope to any who come with questions. Even when it is a hostile charge the reply should not only be positive, stressing the certainty of faith, but gracious, spoken with gentleness and humility.

It is not easy to present the gospel in a convincing way in a culture that has become disillusioned with the traditional Christian faith. The first step, though, is obvious—to stay on center with God himself. The Old Testament prophet Jeremiah, the "praying prophet," puts it this way as he speaks the words of the LORD: "Let not the wise man boast of his wisdom or the strong man boast of his strength or the rich man boast of his riches, but let him who boasts boast about this: that he understands and knows me. . ." (Jeremiah 9:23–24).

We may be busy with religious causes, but if God is a stranger to us, then those pursuits are worth nothing. In fact, we may be so bold to say that God looks at us as objects of such value that he has made knowing us his chief desire. Our love for him is the response to his love for us, and so we give him the best of what we are because he gives us the best of what he is.

Forgetting that everything hinges on the love of God is, in the words of the biblical scholar Geerhardus Vos, "to dereligionize religion at its very core." Proclaiming this central reality in a convincing way begins with being convinced of it ourselves. The other part is of course to tell the Christian story with integrity and persuasiveness.

The gospel story begins with and ends with God; all meaning is in him. In a way, God does not *have* meaning because he *is* meaning. The Creator of the universe, God formed human beings as his image-bearer, ones who can know him, speak with him, and love him. With these privileges come various duties, the first being to comply with God's will for us. This we have failed to do because of our defiance, and as a result the world is corrupted.

It is sometimes difficult to explain why the patterns of this world and human life are so closely bound to our relationship with God, because we see our distress being rooted in natural causes or outside our responsibility. One of the fundamental presuppositions of the Christian worldview, however, is that God gave us a charge, making us accountable for our lives and for the earth. And behind this mandate he gave us the high calling of knowing and trusting him. When that trust is broken, something of the moral structure of the universe is threatened. Our relationships—whether with God, each other, the earth, or even with our own soul—have become broken, dysfunctional, and burdened with liability.

The crucial part of the story is that this dreadful condition has been remedied through God's restitution. In his great love for us the Father sent Jesus Christ to become one of us, and to take the consequences of our condition on himself. By the Holy Spirit, Jesus gives the benefits of his accomplishments to everyone who turns to him in humble faith. At the end of history, the world will be fully renewed with God's peace and justice reigning unimpaired.

Faith is not only knowing the story but embracing it through a whole-souled trust in the God who freely gives us the good news. Believing the gospel does not mean having all the answers, but trusting in a God who has made himself known in the world, our beings, and in a special way in the Bible. The Scriptures are

God's unique and compelling self-disclosure, containing the essence of what we need to know and what we should do.

To believe this message is to come home. Like the prodigal son in Jesus' parable, we are homeless, lost in an alien land, until we come back home to the Father. Or like the elder brother, we may live in the Father's house but because we don't respond to his loving presence with thankfulness, we are as homeless as the prodigal. Much of our contemporary world is alienated from God. The gospel calls it to come home.

TRUTH AND PLAUSIBILITY

The fourth and final approach, which must work together with the first three, is the matter of plausibility. This may seem to be a strange term. Most dictionaries define something as being plausible because "it seems true" as opposed to "it is true." In a courtroom one might hear the prosecutor telling the jury that although the defendant's plea of innocence sounds plausible, it actually is deceptive. But we will use the term in another, more current, way. By plausibility we mean that something is confirmed or made evident and concrete.

Our Lord, telling his followers that he was indeed God, says, "Believe me when I say that I am in the Father and the Father is in me; or at least believe on the evidence of the miracles themselves" (John 14:11). His words should be enough, but if they are not persuasive, they can be confirmed by his deeds. This is truth made visible.

Likewise, in his great prayer recorded in John 17, Jesus indicates that the clear confirmation of God's love for his people is the visible unity of the church (John 17:23). His followers love because he first loved them: "By this all men will know that you are my disciples, if you love one another" (John 13:35). In other words, though truth is valid as it stands, it may be confirmed by clear evidence.

Peter Berger has developed the notion of "plausibility structures." What he means is that knowledge does not occur in the abstract, but is rooted in particular social settings. Certain social structures and institutions make particular ideas easier (or harder) to believe. For example, Marxism is easier to accept in industrial cities than in affluent suburbs. Ice skates sell more quickly in Canada than in Mexico. Similarly, Christian faith is more plausible where the church is strong than where it is weak. To use Berger's language, various institutions "legitimize" belief because they not only reflect it but actually help to reinforce it.

This dimension of plausibility is neither good nor bad; in itself it is quite normal. A good deal of apologetics, however, tends to neglect vital aspects, such as the visible, social, or psychological. At the cost of ineffectiveness, not to mention ignorance of the biblical model, this narrow view presents a more or less purely intellectual statement of the gospel.

In doing apologetics God himself must be a vital part of the process. We have already mentioned the importance of the Holy Spirit's role, but it cannot be stressed too much that the final persuader is not our argument, however well-constructed, but God's Holy Spirit. To be sure, the gospel itself is powerfully persuasive,[5] but there is also power because God's Holy Spirit is at work.[6] Christian discourse is human activity with divine authority.

The Scriptures fully recognize the human need for plausibility and credibility in order to achieve subjective assurance. Paul consistently shows concern that his readers have certainty.[7] We should stress that assurance is not just once-for-all but can be prayed for, developed, nurtured, and even lost, at least temporarily. Assurance comes and goes, and is stronger in some than in others. The variables that account for the degree of certainty a person may have are many.

For those with a legal mind, a preponderance of evidence is the decisive factor in arriving at certainty, which was the case for Frank Morrison. A lawyer and a skeptic, he decided that before he completely dismissed the Christian faith he would take one more look at its central miracle, Christ's resurrection. He examined the evidence, figuring that if he could show this central component to be tenuous, the whole edifice would fall down.

But what he found as he considered the different pieces of evidence—the eye-witness accounts, the historical records, and so on—was that it was one of the most solid cases he had ever encountered. His lawyer's probe guided him to the only honest conclusion, that there was a resurrection of Christ.[8]

For those who have an aesthetic sense, the coherence and beauty of the Christian message may be the convincing element. C. S. Lewis, for example, was drawn to faith through his exposure to the great storytellers. Or for those with more of an interest in psychology, the gospel can be persuasive because of its insights into human personality.

Equally important, certainty can be shattered by various trials or threats to our condition. Sickness, for one, can be the proximate cause for doubting there could be a God who is good. Or another is an awareness of the great and terrible conflicts around the globe. Apologetics will hardly be effective if it stops at logically valid arguments that do not appeal to the hidden fears, frustrations, and personal needs of the hearer.

Doubting can also take more subtle forms as well. For example, many people suffer from the fear that if they believe something it cannot be reliable. This reminds me of a series of jokes based on the remark by Groucho Marx that any club that would have him as a member is one he wouldn't join. Many of us deeply fear being taken in by something that will turn out to be a psychological illusion. Indeed, the fear of credulity is one of the most common obstacles to faith today.

Other kinds of fears hinder certainty as well. For those who are afraid of being ridiculed, assurance comes only when the judgment of God becomes more pressing than the judgment of other people. For those who are ambitious, belief could be hindered by the desire for power.

Plausibility, then, has many forms. It may be psychological, social, or cultural in nature. The point to recognize if we are going to engage in the work of persuasion is that people are more than purely intellectual beings; they have complex dispositions and sensitivities. Instead of being an embarrassment, plausibility structures can be a great asset, as we see in the following example.

James Billington, the Librarian of Congress, has recounted the events of August 1991 when the former Soviet Union saw the final collapse of communism.[9] He was present during the three days that signaled the break up of this powerful modern empire that had tried to eliminate the Christian faith from its territory. Billington notes two forces working to ensure the failure of the hard-liners' last-ditch coup. First were the words of the priests and the believers, many of them older women, who called the people to their Christian roots. New Testaments were also distributed by the Russian Bible Society. Second were the images and metaphors that reinforced those words and contradicted the dominant worldview. Curiously, the color *white* played a significant role. The events began on the Feast of the Transfiguration when Christ, depicted in white robes on the icons, intrudes with his bright light into the dark world. In the "white-stoned" city of Moscow with the White House in the background, the white-haired Yeltsin gave a stirring speech as the people watched the drab soldiers and the dull tanks attempting to gainsay the new freedom. At that moment Christian tradition in the visible and audible forms of priests, believers, Scripture, colors, and icons persuaded the crowd to stand firm against the forces of darkness.

Plausibility and truth are related but are not strictly the same thing. Many arguments are perfect demonstrations of something being valid but not really credible to the audience. An example illustrates: Richard Keyes, Director of l'Abri Fellowship in Massachusetts, teaches a course on cultural apologetics and gives out a particularly difficult assignment. He asks the students to write a paper on a non-Christian thinker, discussing that person's views with a critique and a rebuttal. The students must write about the person they critique in such a way that the thinkers would recognize themselves in the argument.

Many students do poorly on the paper because they lack sympathy, creating and demolishing only a straw man. It is one thing, for example, to show the bankruptcy of French theorist

Jacques Derrida's Deconstruction to those who oppose him, but it is quite another to describe Derrida in a way that he would sense he is being understood.

Thus in doing apologetics we should strive to understand someone's position from within. Our friends should sense that we know why they have come to their conclusions and what they are struggling with, for then our disclosure of the problems will be plausible. And if the disclosure is plausible, chances are the homecoming will be too.

Four Parts of a Whole

Our four principles are not isolated moves on a chess board but belong together and actually require one another. The point of contact is not a sufficient basis for communication. Its correct notion that the unbeliever already knows God must be supplemented by another notion—that the knowledge of God is not assimilated rightly but is tainted by error and pride. Because of this the procedure of disclosure is required, for there must be a way to sort out the different levels of truth and falsity in someone's point of view. But homecoming must follow, for if one only gives a critique without hope it amounts to cruelty. And when one only presents hope without critique the discussion is unrealistic at best and illusory at worst. Finally, none of the three components are of much value unless they are said plausibly and with compassion. The finest apologetic method is of little value unless it hits home.

Keeping the four together is not simply a matter of recalling tactics, but at root is a spiritual matter. Sound and effective apologetic method begins and ends with the worship of God— the very God we present to unbelievers as the only hope for their condition. As we lift up Christ, the best answers will come forth. And that in turn means we have faced our own needs, our own emptiness without God, and we have turned to him and live in his presence. Only when our own reasons of the heart are right can we commend them rightly to others.

Part Two

CONVERSATIONS

6

INITIAL BARRIERS

Surprise is the essence of humor, and nothing is
more surprising than truth.

—Bill Watterson,
The Calvin and Hobbes 10th Anniversary Book, 1995

OBSTACLES AND OPPORTUNITIES

HAVING EXAMINED some of the basic principles and foundations
for apologetics, we come now to its practice. In any given conversation about ultimate questions, the point of contact, disclosure, homecoming, and plausibility should occur throughout. But
it should be stressed that these are not techniques to guarantee
success, because with individual people no single argument nor
certain place to begin will always succeed. The four-fold realities
in the apologetics we have been setting forth, however, should
enable the believer to begin almost anywhere. Although the
gospel is a single truth, bridging the gap between that truth and
the many different peoples and cultures of the world can be done
in many ways, as we will explore in this chapter.

As we will see, all kinds of barriers to faith exist. Often,
because of a particular obstacle in a person's mind, the most difficult moment in a conversation about matters of faith is at the
very beginning. Initial barriers to conversation about spiritual
things can be as formidable as any subsequent ones.

In the examples that follow, we will look at various paths, both positive and negative, that people have traveled in coming to faith, as well as possible ways to help clear the initial ground. The arguments could be used any time, but they are especially appropriate as means to challenge individuals who may be especially difficult to reach for the gospel.[1]

The Wonder of Wonder

Sashi is a Japanese-American musician whose career was planned from a young age, ever since her talent was discovered. Growing up, she did not have much time to think about ultimate spiritual matters. And in the midst of her professional career, when she was not practicing, she would be busy making appointments or taking engagements. A favorite of audiences, she seemed to have a fresh innocence in her playing. In her early professional life she enjoyed a kind of attainment not given to many in her field.

Then in mid-career, Sashi began to have a strange recurring experience so powerful in nature that she was driven to change her routines and take time to study the Bible for the first time in her life. What happened is something many musicians encounter. As Sashi performed certain pieces she began to feel a kind of aesthetic surprise. Although she knew her repertoire thoroughly, every now and then a sense of ecstasy would take over—something wonderful and inexplicable. She began to feel the kind of astonishment she occasionally sensed in her audiences during a particular musical episode, which she had hitherto assumed was caused by her brilliant play. But now she felt it was something more, perhaps something mystical. This strange feeling of amazement caused her to carve out the time she needed to understand the phenomenon and begin a pilgrimage toward the discovery of spiritual truth.

Sashi had confronted the shock of another world that intruded in her own. In her case, as a musician, the intrusion was aesthetic. But the experience of being awakened to discover another reality can happen to anyone.

G. K. Chesterton, an effective apologist, describes his journey to faith in his *Autobiography*. He was exploring the popular outlooks of pessimism and optimism, and was spurred to think about higher things when he began wrestling with an inexplicable sense of gratitude for being alive. He came to the conclusion that real pessimism could never work because to be negative about something one needs a positive standard by which to judge the world. Ironically, pessimism needs optimism to operate.

Chesterton also explored philosophy and found the real problem to be not this or that praiseworthy matter, but praise itself. The quest to understand the "enjoyment of enjoyment" is more difficult than explaining the enjoyment of a particular thing. Soon after this insight Chesterton began to believe.

Both Sashi and Chesterton, in their different ways, were confronted with the problem of goodness. They found themselves delighted with something in life, were grateful, and wanted to thank someone. It drove them to the conclusion that there must be someone to thank. This may not be everyone's experience, but most people at one time or another have encountered the phenomenon of moments of great wonder.

THE LOVE OF GOD IN A DINING ROOM

Sometimes people expect to be hit between the eyes with the supernatural, and failing that, they decide that faith is irrelevant. What may help break through is closely related to the sense of wonder and gratitude—the way in which this world, however ordinary, is a window on things eternal. Christians doing apologetics too often try to impress others with evidences of the bizarre, the miraculous, the supernatural. God truly is Spirit, and leading people to him must entail lifting their horizons to the City of God. But the created world is real, and thus finding God in the ordinary should be as arresting as finding him in a specifically spiritual domain.

Artists and story-tellers such as Cézanne, the brilliant painter of the post-Impressionist period, can often highlight the extraordinary in the ordinary. Although Cézanne is seen as the father of cubism because of his obvious attention to geometrical patterns, a careful examination of his landscapes and still-lifes reveal shapes that emerge from his reading of nature itself. As he saw it, different forms in creation could be translated (not copied) onto the canvas by using such elemental tools as color and light. Rather than drawing abstract figures, he used colors together, chromatically, much like a composer weaves together various melodies and themes, some highlighting others. Cézanne showed how shadows and light could express the form of an object by their ability to accent any of its features.

Writers, too, often reveal the remarkable in the natural. Charles Dickens, for one, shows how strange things can be by peering into the most mundane places. And the great French realists, Honoré de Balzac and Gustave Flaubert, do their best character studies in the most ignoble settings, dramatizing the ultimate issues of life without sermonizing.

Flaubert even reproduces the mood of an epoch in a homely scene in *Madame Bovary*. The despondent Emma Bovary sits in a small room with her husband, surrounded by a smoking stove, a creaking door, humid walls. "With the steam of the boiled beef, there rose from the depths of her soul as it were other inhalations of insipidness. Charles was a slow eater. . . ." Living in the town of Tostes with her commonplace husband is mediocre and without flavor, leading to her despair. Behind her aversion to Charles lies a social critique embedded in the narrative on the bourgeoisie. And behind that is the awareness of the transition from the relatively secure world of pre-revolutionary hierarchy to the uncertain and uncomfortable world of the newly liberated individual.

Flaubert, along with others in the French Restoration, is uncomfortable with characteristics of his period, such as the seething anarchy and the threat of the mob, the lack of a traditional solid theological base, and the growing use of art as a substitute religion.[2] He seeks not to return to the France of former days, but to inspire people to hope for something better. One means he employs toward this aim is his ability to portray a scene as if it were from the eye of God—the compassionate Creator, not a detached deity.

Flaubert's objectivity shows an integral connection of the mundane with all of life, whether in its tragic or comic dimension. The longings of Emma Bovary are the yearnings of an era for more than what the bourgeois culture can offer. Flaubert artfully awakens us to the sadness of a sinful world and the hope of a better one.

SURPRISED BY LAUGHTER

Few things dislodge the complacency of certain skeptics as humor. Closely related to a sense of the extraordinary, humor has an element of mystery that makes it a powerful tool for conversation. Why is a good joke funny? Why do certain animals make us laugh? Why does someone slipping on a banana peel strike us as droll? One reason is that in each of these situations two realms clash—the ideal and the ordinary. We spend much of our lives focused on the ordinary, where life can be sadly dark and meaningless. But at times the other reality intrudes and there is a clash, to which we respond with laughter.

In the classic film *Modern Times*, Charlie Chaplin satirizes the rule of technology. At one point, Chaplin is invited to test a remarkable new eating machine—one that feeds him mechanically without any human effort required. Something inevitably goes wrong, and the robotic arms and dishes become out of synch, food is flying around, and chaos reigns. We laugh at such a scene because the pretensions of modern technology have been shown to be inadequate to the needs of humanity. The ideal realm, where eating is more than a biological function, forces its way into the ordinary sphere of dull technology.

Humor can be cynical and destructive, showing a lack of shame and a loss of honor. Often this negative humor is escapism rather than a reality check. Not only is it an indiscriminate judgment, it is not good humor.

Distrust, which lies at the heart of humor, can work both ways—being a sign of arrogance or a conventionally permissible way to reveal problems. Such literary and dramatic masters as Shakespeare and Cervantes deploy humor through the clown, revealing truth as the two worlds clash. Through humor we can proclaim basic truths about God, sin, and redemption, and even suggest the great surprise of the gospel.

James is one who journeyed toward faith in Christ through humor. He's now an Episcopal priest, but as a young man he was a thoroughgoing skeptic. Though he had been raised in a Christian family, he had had several negative experiences and was turned off by some unattractive Christians. A number of the most outspoken believers he encountered were not consistently living out their faith—some were terrible parents, for instance, and others were dishonest in business dealings. James found that many Christians were, in a word, hypocrites. If the gospel is true, he wondered, how could so many of its adherents be so phony?

What arrested his attention was essentially a joke. On one occasion he raised his objection to Christian belief with a believing friend. After telling his friend that he could not join a religion with so many hypocrites, the Christian turned to James and said there was room for at least one more! This rather elementary quip jolted James into the realization of Augustine's wisdom, that the church is not a museum of saints but a hospital of sinners.

SHOCK TREATMENT

At the other end of the spectrum of ways that people are jolted from their "dogmatic slumbers" are the more negative experiences that intrude upon ordinary life. And the ultimate intrusion, which stymies every ambition and project, is death itself.

Death is certain, but thousands of ways to avoid facing it have been thought up. Some of them are simple forms of denial, such as the worship of youthfulness in Western culture. Other ways are less direct and even ironical. Worrying too much about death, for example, can be a form of denial.

Take Patrick, a slave to the fear of death. His fear showed itself in all kinds of ways: he planned for his "declining" years at the age of thirty-five; moved to a home with only one floor; reserved space in a retirement facility; rarely went out driving; and usually spoke about subjects that betrayed worry, such as the coming stock market crash, the high cost of medical insurance, friends who were ill, or a terrible accident. Sadly, his children grew up feeling they should cater to this fear, and thus tried to protect him from tension of any kind.

Patrick's bondage to fear could not be broken by well-meaning friends or family, for he defused any attempt at rousing him from his narcissism. His brother once wrote him a sharp letter, accusing him of selfishness and wasting his life. His only reply was to his children: "He'll never understand what I am going through. His optimism is shallow—he should try being in my shoes." Others attempted to speak more compassionately, but with no better results.

Then one of his daughters became afflicted with a severe case of cancer of the lymph nodes. She suffered a great deal, and the reality of her pain could not be hidden from her father. Patrick began to worry intensely about her condition, which was not what she needed. As her health went from bad to worse, it became clear that she was dying.

Patrick slowly realized that what his daughter needed could not be achieved by his worry. She needed his help to understand what was happening to her; to know who she was and how to cope with her final weeks. In short, she needed spiritual guidance. He broke out of his shell and began to ask the crucial questions necessary to be of some comfort to his daughter. In his case, the impending death of another person was the occasion for realizing his own condition.

Many of us distinctly remember when it first struck us that we were mortal. For some it is a close brush with danger or sickness. For me, a conference on medical ethics pierced my denial. A speaker was presenting material about genetic engineering and referred in passing to the mystery of death. He noted that although it is easy enough to recognize human death, it is quite another matter to identify what it is or why it happens. This off-hand remark threw me into a dark mood for days. I was in my midthirties and knew intellectually that death would some day greet me, but had never taken the implications very seriously.

OTHER DEATHS

Death comes in many guises. Physical death is the most obvious and most radical, but other "deaths" parallel the reversal that death represents and challenge our assumptions. One such mini-threat, connected to the human life-cycle, occurs when people in their forties experience the midlife crisis. At least two possibilities may lie at the root; the first is not getting what we had hoped for. The great Dr. Samuel Johnson once said, "Man lives not from pleasure to pleasure, but from hope to hope." Often those who invest everything in achieving a certain plateau—in finances, power, or relationships—arrive at midlife only to find their goals unobtained.

Yvette was one who carefully constructed her life. Her natural ambition was fed by the American dream of success and power through hard work and by reading such psychologists as Roger Gould, the Stanford specialist on the human life-cycle. According to Gould, individuals from the age of twenty to midlife need to strive to erase the sense of insecurity of childhood, and one way to become immune to mortality is through achieving wealth and high rank.

After some success but many unfulfilled dreams, Yvette began to reconsider. She had married, but wasn't happy with her marriage or children. After reaching forty she realized there were not ten life times ahead of her. And she also discovered some unmagical qualities about herself, which put into question the whole notion of immunity to death. Angry and resentful for no apparent reason, she began to think of ways to hurt her family and best friends. Finally Yvette began asking some of the big questions about purpose and meaning, began to be grateful for small things, and shed some of her ambition.

The most difficult thing Yvette had to face was her regret over a good deal of wasted time. She had neglected her family, investing everything in a job that was not terribly fulfilling. Only after admitting her own responsibility and guilt for wasting time did she understand that Christ also died for time-wasters.

The second possibility related to the midlife crisis is, ironically, getting what one wants and then feeling it is not worth the effort. There are few more moving testimonies of a sudden awakening in midlife than that of Lee Atwater. Friend and advisor to President Bush and Chairman of the Republican National Committee in the 1980s, he was known for his ruthless means. He justified his actions through a philosophy of nihilism that allowed for the unscrupulous acquisition of wealth and power. But then Atwater contracted cancer and was suddenly eye to eye with the truth. He began to realize the spiritual emptiness of his era, converted to Christ, and in his last few months pleaded with Americans to cure their nation's "tumor of the soul."

Many other forms of death-like experiences can be the occasion for spiritual awakening, such as financial concerns. Annette is an African-American who lives in the inner city and worships each week at a small storefront church. During the sharing time in the service, she would inevitably stand and tell her plight of being afflicted by bureaucracy and financial stress. The power company turned off her electricity. . . . Her landlord will not fix the leaky roof. . . . The neighbors will not lower their music at night. She prays, but doesn't think the Lord hears her.

The Christians in Annette's church were helpful, listening to and praying for her. Her story, however, never changed. Then Annette met Janet, who was in similar straits. On the surface life was not any easier for her friend, yet Janet remained hopeful and seemed to have resources to deal with her afflictions. Over the months Annette began to realize that she had allowed herself to drift subtlety into a form of self-pity, describing the oppression of the power company and the landlord as though they were the cause of every problem. Janet gently led her to consider the larger picture—that ultimately what matters most is a proper relationship with God.

All of these "mini-deaths" can spur someone out of false tranquillity and into dialogue about ultimate matters. Naturally, accounts of coming to faith through the more positive experiences of gratitude and wonder seem more encouraging. But sometimes only the threat of death is effective. Reckoning with death, however, is shock treatment that leads to life only if death itself is properly conceived. Thus it must be accompanied by an awareness of the transcendent.

This has a negative and positive dimension. On the negative side is the reality of heaven and hell—the eternal separation from God and his love. On the positive side, death matters greatly because it ushers in the afterlife. Without opposing death to the reality of hope based in God, confronting death only plunges us into nihilism. But confronting death as it really is— "the last enemy" in the Apostle Paul's definition—will awaken us to consider the real battle for life, which is the battle Christ has waged and won in the spiritual realm against evil.

"WHAT KIND OF MAN IS THIS?"

Finally, a very different approach. When neither the positive encounter with delight nor the negative encounter with death have had an effect, sometimes a direct appeal to some astonishing evidence is the only way people come to faith. Almost anything from biblical history could qualify, but it is best to focus on the centerpiece of the Christian faith, Jesus Christ. He amazes people today, even as he did the disciples who, after watching him rebuke the wind and the waves on the sea of Galilee, asked in wonder, "What kind of man is this?" (Matthew 8:27)

The more honestly one examines Jesus the more difficult it is to define him as anything but what the Bible says he is. Bertrand Russell, the celebrated philosopher and mathematician as well as notorious atheist and libertine earlier in the cen-

tury, often wrote about the dangers of religion. One of his fre-
quent targets was Jesus Christ—the Jesus of the gospels, for Russell did not believe he really existed.[3] Though he admired the
commands to turn the other cheek or not judge, Russell nevertheless saw Jesus as a cruel man because he taught that God
would judge evil-doers and because he berated his enemies as
"vipers." Russell contended that Christ's followers have retarded
all human progress, including racial discrimination, improve-
ments in law, and sexual ethics. He believed that Christianity,
like all religion, is based on fear because it is a concept derived
from Oriental despotisms.

One of the most common mistakes of this view, however, is
that it confuses judgment with malignity. Jesus indeed used the
strongest terms against his enemies. But when reading the New
Testament carefully we see that his enemies are always oppressors
of some kind. "Beware of false prophets," Jesus taught. He was
especially angry when a religious leader misled his followers into
distortions of the will of God.

Bertrand Russell missed two crucial things. The first is that
some moral and spiritual issues cannot simply be cured by paci-
fist toleration. God as the moral arbiter demands a reckoning,
a judgment. Thus the anger and apparent harshness of Jesus are
directed against injustice and cruel oppression and are hardly
indiscriminate. Jesus was ready to forgive where change was in
view. The second gap in Russell's understanding is that Jesus
spoke with unique authority. His words of condemnation—and
his words of love—are not like the words of a wise human leader.

Indeed, the claims of Jesus are so astonishing that it would be
more fitting to call him insane than morally inconsistent. When
a paralyzed man was brought to him for healing, he turned to
him and said, "Son, your sins are forgiven" (Mark 2:5). He was
not pronouncing words of comfort but was actually forgiving the
man's sins. The audience understood his intentions and accused
him of blasphemy.

Nowhere does Jesus claim simply to be a wise human moral
sage. His claims are quite preposterous unless they are true.

Attributing to himself the *I* AM of God's self-disclosure in the Old Testament, he tells his followers "I am the bread of life" (John 6:35). "Before Abraham was born, I am," he answers the Jewish authorities. At his trial the night before his death, the high priest asked him, "Are you the Christ, the Son of the Blessed One?" and Jesus answers, "I am, and you will see the Son of Man sitting at the right hand of the Mighty One coming on the clouds of heaven" (Mark 14:62). The Son of Man is the deity described in Daniel 7:13 who will be the judge of the nations.

Such extravagant language challenges anyone who is ready to dismiss Jesus as only a wise teacher. But are these the words of a madman? Neither do the words themselves nor Jesus' behavior in general qualify as deranged. Leaving aside these extravagant claims, Jesus' moral teachings are in fact sane and wise; his illustrations are drawn from keen observations of life and human habit. He lived openly, refusing to hide behind the odd protective habits that so often characterize insane persons. Audiences frequently testified to his moral character, and in fact one of the criminals crucified next to him exclaimed, "We are punished justly, for we are getting what our deeds deserve. But this man has done nothing wrong" (Luke 23:41).

Of course, much more than his claims, moral perfection, and sanity are attractive and arresting about Jesus. Rather it is the wonder of his understanding of human nature; his single-minded purpose; the extraordinary way in which he fulfills the Old Testament prophecies and typological figures; his compassion; his ability to discuss any issue, identifying the heart of a matter; the drama of his sufferings, persecution, and death; the reality of his resurrection.

According to Christian teaching, Jesus is the God-man who came to earth in order to obey God where we had failed to do so, die for sins for which we could not atone, and rise victorious over evil, ushering in a new world where peace and justice will reign. An honest appraisal of him can come to no other conclusion.

7

BEYOND BELIEF

As we get ready to tell the person God's answer to his or her need, we must be sure that the individual understands that we are talking about real truth, and not something vaguely religious which seems to work psychologically.

—Francis A. Schaeffer,
The God Who Is There, 1968

THE CHARGE OF AN ILLUSION

One of the most haunting questions facing seekers, and one not foreign to believers, is whether faith is so motivated by human needs that it has no real basis in truth. Those who believe the Christian faith to be an illusion often quip that religion is a crutch. Whether a derisive comment or a serious question, the issue is important not only because we want faith to be based on facts but also because credulity is so harmful.

To arrive at a satisfactory answer we will look at the more thoughtful and serious advocates of the view that faith is illusory. Though few people would qualify as true atheists, the arguments put forth by some of the more notorious ones in recent history are clear, giving us the opportunity to examine the basic issues in a succinct manner.

In 1842, German philosopher Ludwig Feuerbach wrote a short essay that had an enormous impact. Its title, "Preliminary

Theses on the Reform of Philosophy,"[1] parodies Martin Luther's famous Ninety-Five Theses, posted on the door of Wittenberg University over three hundred years before. In it, Feuerbach called his contemporaries to finish the job of exposing religion for what it really was, merely a projection. He was dramatic, declaring in the opening sentence: "The secret of *theology* is *anthropology*." Thus Feuerbach claimed that whenever people believe in God or any other basic religious tenet, they are only projecting their own nature.

Karl Marx, partly inspired by this manifesto but taking a different tack, declared that religion is "the opium of the people." Whereas for Feuerbach the illusion is a cognitive error, for Marx it is a drug that distracts from the need to reform society. Religion is therefore ideology—a means to serve the interests of the powerful. It is important to notice that Marx was neither particularly interested in the content of religion nor bent on arguing against specific doctrines. Rather he saw it as phenomenon that could be manipulative.

In our own century Sigmund Freud joined this school of thought in his distinct way. He wrote powerfully that religion, like art and philosophy, is a projection by means of which we rid ourselves of guilt. In *The Future of an Illusion*[2] he argues that civilization imposes rules for behavior that conflict with our instincts. A regrettable necessity, civilization uses religion to make life bearable by putting a somewhat human face on the otherwise dangerous natural surroundings of human existence. Belief in God, Freud claims, began as a way to posit a beneficial force behind the chaos of the world; though that makes us feel secure, it is profoundly unscientific and therefore illusory—caused by wishes and needs. In contrast, science and its adjunct psychoanalysis is the only objective approach to life, being far better than religion at liberating humanity and providing for sound morals.

Still more recently, this notion has become even more radical. French thinkers Michel Foucault, Jacques Derrida, and the so-called Deconstructionists, better known in academic circles than outside, believe that not only religion is illusory. They consider the notion of truth itself a dangerous doctrine of the European Enlightenment, a weapon of the oppressor class. As a form of "intellectual terrorism," truth, like religion, is a hypocrisy—a pretension that leads to arbitrary uses of power. Religion claims there is something unitary and absolute, which, say these philosophers, cannot but lead to cruelty.

Admittedly, all these "masters of suspicion" who are so well-schooled in the "art of mistrust" may not represent the common person's doubts about truth. But in order to sort out the issues it helps to examine a sharper position; in doing so we'll apply the twin principles of disclosure and homecoming. Without being exhaustive, we can look at a few responses.

CONFESSION IS GOOD FOR THE SOUL

Before we answer the atheist's objection, it is important to acknowledge something they have right—that religion often is an illusion. Sadly, we human beings are very gifted in self-deception; we can talk ourselves into believing almost anything. Alcohol abusers, for instance, can convince themselves that they have no problem, that they can always refuse a drink. Denial is the doorway to their illusion. Is it not the same with religious believers, including Christians? Do we not often go to church, pray, and take the sacraments without faith? In doing so we are "religious" without being "Christian."

One of the most prevalent warnings in the Scriptures is against those who think they are pleasing God by their religion but are not. The prophet Amos reports God's strong words to denounce the worship of Israel: "I hate, I despise your religious feasts; I cannot stand your assemblies. . ." (Amos 5:21). Our Lord himself warned that many would proclaim their record of religious deeds on the last day but he would reply, "I never knew you. Away from me you evildoers!" (Matthew 7:23)

Not only do we not need Feuerbach, Marx, and Freud to tell us about the dangers of idolatry; their own ideas are actually derived from a biblical critique of idolatry. So obviously those of us inside the church can be lured by this kind of deception just as those outside it, and it can take many forms. There have been theological rationalizations for slavery, colonial domination, and the subjugation of women to name a few. Almost any doctrine can be taken out of context to foster injustice. Using the Christian themes of providence, diversity, and patience, not only have people justified the unequal treatment of different minority groups but also, to use the Marxian metaphor, have been drugged into deceiving themselves that it is the will of God.

WHOSE ILLUSION IS IT?

Only after reckoning honestly with distorted religion through the biblical critique of idolatry and the attacks of thoughtful atheists can we turn to find the falsity in atheism itself. The deep flaws are indeed there, and need to be identified. The most basic is the refusal of the atheists to admit that they too have a religious bias. Branding religion as anthropology, opium, illusion, or terrorism can work both ways. What assurance do we have that atheists are not nurturing an illusion after all? Anyone can claim to be objective and pass others through the grid of their worldview. But what about the foundation of that so-called objectivity? Is it not just as religiously established as the worldview of theism?

A revealing section toward the end of Freud's *The Future of an Illusion* exposes the dilemma. If he is right and religion is an illusion, then what guarantees that his own view—the truth of "science"—is not itself an illusion? Freud is aware of this irony: "But I will moderate my zeal and admit the possibility that I, too, am chasing an illusion." He hastily adds that he is willing to wait until his view is exonerated and tellingly decides that he will "trust the *god* of reason," which will some day "liberate humanity from its weaknesses."[3] This is an extraordinary moment in the literature of atheism—not only can Freud not escape a religious commitment, but his language is revealingly theological!

Through the tactic of disclosure we discover that arguments for faith as projection can simply be turned on their head. More is involved than just a self-refuting contradiction; the strategy of disclosure is once again based on the assurance of the point of contact. All people are religious, as we have argued, whether they wish to be or not. Atheists have a god that helps them push back the revelation of the true God they are confronted with every day. Their god may serve to keep them from despair or provide fulfillment in a confusing world. But it is a god nevertheless, one constructed in the same old "idol factory" of the human heart as all our idols. The burden of proof is on the atheist to show why science is objective and authoritative truth and why religion is illusion. In fact, as Freud began to anticipate, science may be the biggest crutch going.[4]

Similarly, when answering the radical diagnoses of Foucault, Derrida, or others who believe truth to be oppressive, we can also humbly begin to ask if their philosophy is not an illusion. As with Freud, many of the most radical Deconstructionists have a need to appeal to something positive, something quasireligious, to put in the place of what they have torn down. Tellingly, critic Richard Rorty advocates textual study as *therapy*, a kind of practical way to heal the wounds of criticism. Derrida champions *ethics* as the new way to steer clear of literary despair.

ARE DREAMS WRONG?

The tactic we have called disclosure often involves this sort of "neutralizing" or turning an argument on itself. The next step—homecoming—is to show that although religion can be construed to be oppressive or illusory, all belief is not for that reason invalid. The misuse of one thing does not make every use illegitimate. For example, although various cults or sects quote passages of the Bible out of context, this hardly makes the Bible invalid.

Similarly, the presence of illusory needs and wishes does not mean that all needs and wishes are misguided. The need for God is so prevalent in people all over the world that, rather than being a problem, it is more likely a sign that such a God exists after all. We should not be embarrassed about our religious needs and longings as though they were a sign of weakness. Rather they are the marks of our dignity, made as we are as God's image-bearers.

C. S. Lewis pointed out that the deep longing characteristic of human beings—the longing for another world and for meaning and value—is not inimical to Christian faith but highly compatible with it. The common yearning for another world is a good sign that there may be such a world. Our hope in an afterlife is a clue to there being an afterlife.

Of course, needs in themselves are multifaceted; we need to be painfully honest about motives. Doubts about God's existence are submerged in all kinds of layers that can cloud our understanding. People may doubt God's goodness because they had a cruel father, because they don't trust their perception, or because they are trying to escape their commitments.

However complex someone's uncertainty may be, there is, if the Christian faith is true, something deeply wrong with doubting God's presence. Despite apparent contradictions, the evidence points to his reality and goodness. Everything points to God, from the world to the self to world cultures to the Bible. We need the "reasons of the heart," faith seeking understanding, to find him fully and to interpret correctly the knowledge we already possess.

8

ONE WAY? NO WAY?

> A society in which any kind of nonsense is
> acceptable is not a free society. An agnostic
> pluralism has no defense against nonsense.
> —Lesslie Newbigin, *Truth to Tell*, 1991

THE MOST PREPOSTEROUS CLAIM

FEW SERIOUS CONVERSATIONS about the Christian faith last long
before the question is raised: How can there be only one truth?
This quandary has a number of variations. At one end, the issue
is how we can know anything at all with certainty: What ground
is there for the very possibility of knowing God or anything else
to be true? At the other end is the issue of exclusivity: Cannot
the Christian faith be one among many valid faith beliefs? Are
people who have never heard the gospel condemned? Can they
be saved without an articulate faith in Christ?

Adjunct questions are often raised as well. Isn't the claim
to exclusive truth by definition arrogant? Don't missionaries
impose their views on others, impinging their freedom? What
about the rise of fundamentalism—isn't it intolerant at best and
dangerous at worst? In a given society, can we not all live
together without having to worry about religion?

These questions are likely to be more prominent in our era
than they were prior to the rise of modernity. Indeed, one of the
main features of that mode of civilization is *pluralism*, which

refers to the coexistence of groups and institutions that have major differences. Never before have people from so many backgrounds and cultures been thrust together. Owing to rapid communication, easy transportation, and an increasingly global economy, we live and work side by side with people from horizons distinct from our own. Were we living in the Middle Ages, chances are we would not encounter more than a hundred different people during our entire lifetime, most of them resembling us. Today, however, we encounter hundreds if not thousands of people each day, and, despite certain boundaries that reinforce similarity, our neighbors do not resemble us.

No wonder, then, that it is difficult to believe there could only be one truth. The claim does not so much defy logic as it does observation—we look at the different kinds of people surrounding us and naturally wonder how any one group could be right. When I was searching for truth as a young man, the question of the exclusivity of the gospel was a principal stumbling block for me. Most Christians I met told me to disregard the issue, saying it was surely just a smokescreen hiding my more basic personal needs.

TRUTH'S REQUIREMENTS

When the question is asked, "How can the Christian faith be the only truth when there are so many other religions?" it is important to find out what is behind the query. One person may see it as unfair that only one segment of humanity should know the truth. Of the nearly six billion people on earth, possibly two billion are Christians. How can two-thirds of humanity be wrong about something so important? To that objection we have a twofold reply: First, if Christianity is true, no one is without some light, either from the external world or the conscience.[1] Although unbelievers may not have processed the information correctly, they have enough to be held accountable. Second, truth is not determined democratically—decisions about truth are not based on the majority's beliefs. Often a small minority can be right and the many others wrong. For example, although in many cultures around the world women are considered inferior to men, that does not make it right.

Another person may think it inappropriate for Christians to impose their views on others. It is indeed an error to impose religious convictions on others if by imposition is meant the forcible, manipulative foisting of certain doctrines on other people. Followers of Christ should be the first to denounce this, whether in the sad historical examples of conquerors requiring official adherence to their own brand of religion or in current times.

But Christians, although not forcing others to believe as they do, simply cannot refrain from proclaiming the truth or persuading others. We do not believe we have invented the truth, but rather we see how far from the truth we have been and want to share God's revelation with others. Christ is the door to eternal life, and we want others to discover the same liberation we have.

One reason it can be difficult to accept the idea of truth in our contemporary setting is that we tend to see religious verity as a private or subjective matter. We often say that others may believe what they wish as long as we can believe what we wish. But we should not want to push this too far—in the extreme it would mean that school teachers could not teach math, judges could not adjudicate, and parents could not inculcate. But, one would argue, those things are objective whereas religion is so personal.

To be sure, a development in the West with roots in the Romantic movement has equated religious conviction with feelings. Since the nineteenth century in particular the great poets and musicians have considered religious sentiment to be an inexpressible sign of the human capacity for the divine. To disturb that sentiment is considered somehow indecent, something like interrupting someone's enjoyment of a beautiful sunset. In one way, religious piety does have a very private side—in times of prayer and meditation, we may enjoy a certain intimacy with

God that is hard to make public. But we shouldn't confuse religion with our feelings, for at times convictions must oppose personal feelings that are misleading.

Yet a third person may have something else in mind when asking the question of the truths of other faiths. One common presupposition behind the question is that at bottom all religions are the same; specifically that there is one great Truth (capital T) and many little truths (small t) leading to it. Each religion may have its particular set of rituals, symbols, and holy persons, but the adherents will eventually find a universal truth that transcends all the particular symbols and practices.

This approach has serious flaws, the main one being that it lumps all religions into one paradigm. All are said to begin at the same level, and all will reach the same place. But a careful look at different worldviews makes it impossible to be so categorical. Try looking for a basic commonality in worldviews. It is not a belief in God because not all worldviews believe in God—Confucianism is agnostic; Zen Buddhism atheistic. Nor is it the authority of a sacred text, for not all religions have such texts, and those that do are not comparable. The Vedas do not have the same status as the Koran. The inspiration for the Bible is quite distinct from the way the *Bhagavadgita* was handed down. Nor is it an eschatology—a vision for the end of the world. Marxism's vision is based on historical materialism but refuses the label "religion." Mahayana Buddhism believes in abandoning any utopian ideas and opting for the sunyata, or ultimate void. The list continues. When all is said and done, what finally matters is one essential question: Is it true?

ALL OR NOTHING?

It is important to underline that Christians acknowledge the truth in other religions. Believing that the basics of truth and salvation are found in biblical revelation, culminating in Jesus Christ, does not mean believing that only Christians have truth or wisdom. Those who have spent time with Islamic cultures, for example, know their great insights that in many cases put Westerners to shame, such as respect for a guest, reverence for a sacred text, and rigorous standards for scholarship.

Christians can be insensitive to the riches offered in other worldviews. But of course it is the case that if the gospel is true, there must be serious flaws in other positions. It is not our purpose here to review different religions and assess their strengths and weaknesses, but rather to plead for an honest appreciation of the strengths of other positions while examining the fundamental problems.

Living in southern France for many years, my family and I were exposed to many Muslims and learned much about Islam's numerous insights and serious flaws. Islam is monistic in doctrine—God is one, not many. The Koran, rather than God's person and love, is the one rule for all of life, revealing what to do and believe. According to the Koran, God is Almighty but cannot be known as a person; he is not "Father." The "Will" of Allah is more often an ironclad fate than loving providence. Life is highly regulated and everything, including eating, is subject to strict law. For many sects within Islam, conquest and rule are the only ways to establish this way of life.

At heart, Islam holds to a legalistic worldview. One must live with the terrible burden of having to keep strictly to the law for fear of being condemned by Allah. According to Islamic lore, people are each born with two angels assigned to them, one sitting on the left shoulder and recording all the evil thoughts, words, and deeds, and the other sitting on the right shoulder and recording all the good thoughts, words, and deeds. At the end of life an accounting is made, but there is no way to know whether one's good deeds will outweigh one's sins of omission and commission on the day of judgment. Above all, there is no atonement for sin and no assurance of God's personal love.

As with Islam, the burden of self-liberation is at the core of many of the world religions. There are many different versions, from the karma of Hinduism to the tao of Lao Tze. But no matter how many good deeds we may accomplish, we can never erase our guilt and moral liability against God.

The Christian faith is actually unique in its view of what is wrong and what can be done. The diagnosis, translated by the words sin and guilt, is that our separation from God and the ensuing distress is caused by a moral declaration of independence. The only remedy is for God himself to intervene, which he did by becoming a man and suffering the consequences of our sin and guilt. Coming back to God is a matter of lifting up empty hands, trusting that Christ's work is effectual.

Various non-Christian religions may have many virtues, but at the deepest level they cannot make atonement and thus cannot truly lead one to God. This is sobering thought, but if the gospel of Christ is right in this ultimate and deepest sense, then other religions cannot be as well. Two contradictory philosophies simply cannot both be valid. It is not arrogant to believe this, but humbling. Being a Christian should actually make us extremely modest because we have come to terms with the sobering reality of our condition: helplessness. The gospel may not be flattering, though it is liberating.

IS CHRIST THE ONLY WAY?

We can come at the question of uniqueness in another way, by considering Jesus Christ. How could a first-century Palestinian Rabbi be "the way, the truth, and the life" for all peoples, including those from very different social and religious backgrounds? And can a tan-colored person be the savior of blacks? Can a male adequately represent women? Can someone with a stable family sympathize with someone whose family has abused them? The list could go on. We shall consider two levels of resolution.

First, the traditional theology of the church, explicating the Scriptures, holds strongly that Jesus is both a man with all the particularities of his race and simultaneously God himself. One of the most classic formulations says he is one person in two natures, human and divine. If it is difficult to imagine that a first-century

Jew could save the whole world, consider that it was no mere man facing death on the cross. When Jesus looked up and cried out, "My God, my God, why have you forsaken me?" this was the agony of God, not simply the suffering of a man.

Because people are at fault, only a person could appropriately bear the responsibility and consequences for humanity's guilt. But only God can endure it. One of the most basic ways to explain Christ's atonement is in the language of penal substitution. According to the standards of divine justice, we who are guilty owe a debt to God, much as on the human level a criminal owes a debt to society. Because we are incapable of paying the debt, someone else has to, and the only one who can is someone not in a position of deficit, a person moreover capable of paying everyone else's debt. That person is God. The Westminster Shorter Catechism puts it succinctly:

> Q. 14. Can any mere creature make the payment for us?
> A. No one. First of all, God does not want to punish any other creature for man's debt. Moreover, no mere creature can bear the burden of God's eternal wrath against sin and redeem others from it.
>
> Q. 15. Then, what kind of mediator and redeemer must we seek?
> A. One who is a true and righteous man and yet more powerful than all creatures, that is, one who is at the same time true God.[2]

If Christ is the God-Man (Anselm of Canterbury's timeless expression), then it cannot be someone else, nor can the answer to human debt be remedied in any other way. There can only be one way to salvation.

Second, though Jesus did not suffer every kind of trial nor undergo every different human experience, what he did endure was truly typical for humanity. The book of Hebrews is a study of Christ as a priest—one who bears people's burdens, makes intercession, and becomes the sole surrogate for sin. The author argues that Christ can be this priest because of his experience as a man. "Because he himself suffered when he was tempted, he is able to help those who are being tempted" (Hebrews 2:18). As a result, we have an intermediary who understands us and can help us in our own need. "For we do not have a high priest who is unable to sympathize with our weaknesses, but we have one who has been tempted in every way, just as we are—yet without sin. Let us then approach the throne of grace with confidence, so that we may receive mercy and find grace to help us in time of need" (4:15–16).

Christ, then, is uniquely able to help us because he suffered and was tempted but never capitulated. How is Christ our help in time of need, when the need is cancer? Or war? Or the death of a child? Again, as the great priest, he not only stands by us to sympathize and comfort but paves the way for an ultimate relief from our afflictions. And mysteriously, when we suffer we participate in the name of Christ in a special way—we share the privilege of suffering as he once did. As Peter the Apostle put it, "Dear friends, do not be surprised at the painful trial you are suffering, as though something strange were happening to you. But rejoice that you participate in the sufferings of Christ, so that you may be overjoyed when his glory is revealed. . . . [I]f you suffer as a Christian, do not be ashamed, but praise God that you bear that name" (1 Peter 4:12–13, 16).

Because Christ is unique, so is the way to deal with adversity. We do not escape trials as Christians, but we do have a singular way to endure them and know that our high priest will ultimately remove every hardship and injustice. As the great singer Blind Willy Johnson says in one of his songs, "Take your burden to the Lord and leave it there. Leave it there. Leave it there."

Thus Jesus is able to represent every kind of human being. It may seem strange to modern ears to hear that a person from a particular culture and race, a specific economic and social background, a male and a celibate, could represent rich and poor, men and women, African and Asian. But if the idea of representation is at all valid, the person who is my priest is necessarily different from me but can understand me because he has experienced the same sorts of difficulties I have. Jesus therefore cannot be our representative if he is only a spirit or a philosophical abstraction; he must be a human who can empathize with the circumstances of so many different people.

Celebrating Diversity

Finally, a brief word about the other side of our topic in this chapter. Ironically, while we resist suggestions that somehow all religions are the same and that Christ is one of many saviors, at the same time we should applaud diversity as such. God made the world wonderfully diverse; humanity itself is rich with cultural, ethnic, and physical differences. These are not an embarrassment but a great tribute to the Creator, who is himself "three in one."

Even though diversity can turn into fragmentation and rivalry in a fallen and broken world, we must not abandon its virtues. It may seem on the surface that any kind of pluralism is at odds with the singleness of truth. In a world where moral values and theological truths are considered matters of personal preference, it is understandable that to some Christians any pluralism is considered threatening. But pluralism, at least as I am using the term, refers to the fact of social and cultural diversity with both good and bad facets.

In itself, diversity of peoples and races reflects God's own diversity. And in our fallen world some of that diversity is problematic, resulting from sin. The word "heresy," for example, might seem old-fashioned, but it basically means "choice" with the connotation of deliberately choosing to deviate from the right path. This kind of diversity is not normal and in the end will not hold together.

Nevertheless, much of our diversity is good and enriching. Christians should not feel threatened by cultural differences, but in fact should be leading the charge in commending variety because we know from the creation itself that God loves to paint from a many-colored palette.

Our age is particularly sensitive to the question of diversity. There is often more heat than light when it comes to the claims of one religion to be exclusive. It is true that at the most basic level the Christian faith is incomparable. It is simply not possible for Christ to have paved the way to God if other ways can also be valid. If the gospel is true, there is a fundamental incompatibility between belief and unbelief. Yet at the same time nothing in the Scripture teaches that Christians cannot get along with others. And furthermore, the gospel message carries with it a genuine celebration of diversity within the unity of the faith. Not only are barriers broken down between Jew and Gentile, men and women, employer and employee, but the legitimate ethnic, racial, and gender differences are preserved.

9

THE GREAT OUTRAGE

> We may observe how the Scriptures protest against all independent analyses of the world which leave God, even though temporarily, in the shadows. The decision of faith, which knows from the start that any unrighteousness in God is impossible, is decisive for any consideration of theodicy.
> —G. C. Berkouwer, *The Providence of God*, 1955

EVIL IS NOT A PROBLEM

EVIL IS NOT A PROBLEM, it is *the* problem—the ultimate unreasonable reality and what ought not to be. So many questions that confront us in apologetic conversation eventually focus on defending God against the charge of malevolence: How can God be good and there be evil? Is there a devil? Are we really free? Is there collective guilt? Is there any purpose to suffering? And though the problem of evil has a theoretical side, it is not primarily abstract; it includes the pain of losing a loved one, the puzzle of an innocent victim, or danger, disease, and death itself.

Suffering, which is often the most obvious form of evil, defies the will. The French poet Baudelaire wrestles with its power: "Behave, oh my pain," he says to the unwanted friend. Pain in itself has no meaning, but it requires a context before it can be called suffering. The cross of Christ is among other things the greatest symbol of the bond between pain and suffering, showing them to be visible and inescapable. It is the ultimate injustice, the death of the innocent one. It also is the symbol of love and compassion, for on it the righteous died for the unrighteous, light penetrating darkness. No wonder that the cross has been the preeminent sign for artists, chaplains, and theologians who confront the deepest problems of humanity.

Thus it is no surprise that all philosophies and religions are preoccupied with evil, suffering, and pain; the problem of evil is not specially a Christian problem. Those who struggle with evil have recognized that something is good and right, and yet things have gone wrong. Anyone who has a "problem" of evil admits to a standard, and thus to the need to reconcile the reality and the standard.

Three basic and interrelated questions have preoccupied the best minds throughout the ages. The first is the origin of evil: How did it get here? Does it have a purpose? If God is good, then how did evil penetrate into the universe? The second regards the nature of evil: What is it? Is it a substance, a state, or a counterreality? The third concerns the solution. What can be done? Do we ignore it or endure it? Is there victory over it?

Although a brief chapter will not answer these questions completely, we will set out the various positions on the problem of evil, evaluate their strengths and weaknesses, and then make three affirmations regarding the three basic questions.

THE SCHOOL OF SUFFERING

Sheldon Van Auken's *A Severe Mercy* is a love story with a powerful message about the purpose of suffering. "Davy" is the young woman Sheldon meets in a department store, falls in love with, and then marries. Worlds upon worlds open up to them as they discover how much they share, including a common search for truth. To protect their relationship they decide to keep up a "shield of love," a kind of protective barrier against all assaults. Children, they decide, would be intruders, and so they do not have any.

At one point they go to Oxford University to study, where they meet some Christians, including C. S. Lewis. Davy eventually becomes a believer, which poses problems at first since Sheldon had not yet found faith. The shield is threatened until he too becomes a Christian and all is well.

But then Davy contracts terminal cancer. With great force, Van Auken describes the terrible pain, physical and psychological, and the death of his beloved wife. Then comes the real drama. Sheldon experiences the many phases of grief—anger, bargaining, and resignation. During this time he is most comforted and challenged by letters from C. S. Lewis, through which he realizes that losing Davy is a "severe mercy" because she is now whole and that which they had both longed for is now hers. Lewis also helped him to understand that their love had been too ingrown. He chided Sheldon for robbing Davy of motherhood. It had been "us and God," rather than "God and us." In a way, through death, their love was saved.

On the positive side, who cannot recognize that evil is a teacher? We often learn through suffering what we could not have learned otherwise. Improvement by affliction is a theme in the Scriptures. Remember Joseph, sold into slavery by his jealous brothers, who yet becomes the dispenser of food in Egypt during a terrible famine. When his brothers face him, he is able to say, "You intended to harm me; but God intended it for good to accomplish what is now being done, the saving of many lives" (Genesis 50:20). The cross of Christ is the preeminent example of redemption through and because of evil.

On the negative side, however, the redemptive use of evil will never do as an *explanation* for evil. It is one thing to make use of evil for good once it exists, but it is quite another to create it in the first place. Some believe the repulsive idea that God made evil in order to bring about a greater good. The Bible often denounces such an idea: He is the holy one; in him is no shadow of turning; he can never tempt anyone.

A particular medieval theology takes this view, celebrating the "felix culpa," the happy guilt of Adam's fall. Because of it

Christ's redemption could occur. But this notion is utterly unbiblical—guilt is never happy, and though sometimes God brings good out of bad, celebrating evil is a loathsome notion.

IT'S ALL A DREAM

A second theory of evil with many versions claims that it is illusory. According to philosophic Hinduism only the Brahman is real, and everything else is a "passage" from the center to the outermost reaches. Existence is cyclical, moving from the manifest to the nonmanifest, from force to matter, from energy to substance. What we call evil is actually *maya*—illusion, dream, deception. Any idea that we suffer is connected to the fantasy that we are human, that we matter, that we have rights and feelings.

Western versions abound as well. Philosopher Charles Werner says evil comes from the dissociation of desire (which is connected to things) and intelligence (which is able to control life). In such pseudo-Christian views as Christian Science, evil, including suffering and disease, is not real but is connected with the physical world, which exists at a great distance from the spiritual world. Some approaches to the Christian life take a somewhat similar view, saying that to be concerned about suffering is unspiritual. Other popular examples can be seen in the Victorian ethic of "the stiff upper lip" or the macho bravery of the "tough guy."

Again, this view has something to commend it. There is indeed something less than ultimate, something not quite real about evil. Augustine in his polemics against the Manichaeians stressed that evil is not a *thing*—it is insubstantial. Unlike good, which is self-defining, evil needs good in order to make sense. In his famous phrase, evil is *privatio boni*, a privation, an absence.

His understanding is helpful against all views that make evil into something substantial. Evil is not in food, but in the gluttonous way we abuse it. It is not in the chords and rhythms of music, but in the way we use them for self-indulgence. There is theological insight in calling evil the absence of good, for it draws attention to the Father of Lights, the God by whose attributes we define everything else. In the history of redemption, too, evil is transitory. The Apostle Paul tells us the "present sufferings are not worth comparing with the glory that will be revealed in us" (Romans 8:18).

But evil is not just the absence of something else, it is a dreadful reality. In addition to being transgressive, evil has a "hideous strength" that not everyone experiences personally or directly. Sometimes the discovery of the suffering of other people can have a deep impact. Marie Moscovici, the French psychoanalyst, came to terms with the reality of evil when she subjected herself to the nine-hour film *Shoah* by Claude Lanzman. Most of it she endured without any identifiable emotion, except for one episode when Jews were transferred from Terezin to Auschwitz. They did not suspect their dreadful fate until minutes before being gassed, when they began to sing the Jewish *Hymn to Hope*. Moscovici burst into uncontrollable tears and somehow knew, especially because of the music, that evil had a face and that it was her pain as well as theirs. [1]

The Scriptures never treat evil as an illusion. Jesus himself, God though he be, was "a man of sorrows" and "acquainted with grief." An astonishing episode in the gospel of John records an encounter of Jesus with evil (John 11:1–44). Lazarus, Mary's brother and Jesus' close friend, died. As Jesus saw Mary grieving and as he thought about his friend, twice the text says, "he was deeply moved in spirit" (vv. 33, 38). The Greek is actually the strongest term for anger, literally meaning that Jesus groaned with fury. When the account adds, "Jesus wept," the implication is not sentimental regret but the weeping of outrage. Jesus, the creator of the universe, Jesus who would shortly raise Lazarus from the dead, Jesus the wholly other, is furious at death, *without* being angry at himself. He made the world without evil; it entered in as an alien intruder. Thus evil, not God, is the real enemy.

Of course, Jesus was no stranger to suffering and evil. After this incident he would go to Jerusalem and one week later die a dreadful death, "so that by the grace of God he might taste death for everyone" (Hebrews 2:9). Christians who imagine they are somehow exempt from the afflictions common to humanity are sadly mistaken. Christ did not say he would relieve us from plight, but he said something much more hopeful: "In this world you will have trouble. But take heart! I have overcome the world" (John 16:33).

It's Just the Way Things Are

A third view appeals to universal order, with good and evil as somehow necessary and coexisting. One variant of this view that is easiest to identify, though it rarely occurs in a pure form, is dualism. The early church struggled with a heresy known as Manichaeism, which sees two absolute principles in the universe—Light, personified in the Father of Lights, and Darkness, personified in the Prince of Darkness. Manichaeism's main legacy is the idea that good and evil are equal, or nearly equal, forces.

An influential version of this is the "imperfect of the good," when the presence of evil is seen as somehow necessary in the order of things. The classic expression of this tradition is the eighteenth-century philosophy known as optimism, whose two most famous proponents are G. W. Leibnitz and Alexander Pope. The basic idea is that the world is organized as a vast chain of being. From the highest (God) to the lowest (nonbeing), every part of the world, including humanity, fits in a rational system. Evil is a necessary part of the order of things, the underside of the good. In his *Essay on Man*, Pope pleads, "Then say not Man's imperfect, Heaven at fault; Say rather, Man's as perfect as he ought." His epic ends with the affirmation, "And, spite of Pride, in erring Reason's spite, One truth is clear, whatever is, is right."

To its credit, dualism takes evil seriously. The devil is a real person, not simply a vague symbol. The particular form of optimism also celebrates the wisdom of God, calling us to recognize, with Job, that though we do not have all the answers sometimes reasons for evil exist that fit into God's good plan. The popular image of the tapestry is often used to say that confusion reigns on the side of human perception, but in the end we will see everything as God does—a beautiful design.

On the debit side, however, the great problem of any view that assigns evil to the order of things is that God necessarily becomes the author of evil. However much his wisdom is applauded, at best, proponents of this view have to admit that God could not do otherwise than to foster evil—meaning that either he is not altogether good or that he is not altogether powerful.

Perhaps the main problem is that evil somehow is seen as necessary. But that makes it explicable, and so it really amounts to a justification—an excuse.

THE RISK OF FREEDOM

One of the most popular views among modern Christians believers is that although God is the creator he did not create evil but rather the *possibility* of evil, because without it there could be no guarantee of freedom. The idea is that God created humanity in order to love him. But coerced love is not true love, so he endowed the race with freedom to choose for him or against him. As the argument goes, when the wrong choice was made, God was not responsible. He may have planted the possibility of evil in us, but not evil itself. Further, God could have forced us to stay good, but he voluntarily gave up some of his power in order to ensure human autonomy.

The virtue of this approach is to put the blame for evil squarely on human beings, not on God nor on the order of things. The fall occurred not because of any present program nor some seed of discord in the creation.[2] The world was created good. At the same time, God is not only all-powerful and all-knowing, but is willing to make sacrifices for the love of his world. He respects the reality of creation and is willing to let secondary causes and natural laws do their work without his interference. Besides this, freedom is a precious value that gives responsibility. Unlike the view that evil is illusion, evil is real, though the fault of the human beings who chose it.

Attractive as it may be, this view has serious defects. The principal one is its inability to safeguard God's innocence after all. Despite putting the emphasis on human responsibility, God is still involved, because it was he that placed the alternative to choose evil in the scheme. When we think of it, what is *possibility*? Is it not a mechanism whereby the undesirable can still happen? If I decide to drive at 100 m.p.h. on a mountain road and pass the slower car in front of me on a curve, not seeing ahead, I may be taking a relatively safe risk. The chances of another car coming toward me may be remote. But if a collision occurs, I cannot very well blame "possibility"; I am responsible for taking the risk. Similarly, if God creates a world that is quite safe from evil yet includes a risk that it be introduced, he is ultimately to blame.

The problem with this view becomes even clearer when we look at its corollary, the humility of God. The scheme has it that God relinquishes some of his power in order to make sure human beings are not coerced. This sounds fine until we wonder what is a God who is less than all-powerful. Can God be God if he does not control all things?

This raises the matter of divine control and human freedom. The best solution is to say that both are mysteriously true— God's determining all things and human free agency. We can leave the enigma open because we know there is an answer, even though we are not able to rationalize it.

An illustration may help. When a friend is ill, two measures commend themselves, prayer and medicine. If we pray but do not remedy we are wrongly spiritual; if we bring cures but do not implore the Great Physician we are wrongly materialistic. How can both be right? We simply have no way of knowing. It is no use trying to establish human freedom by saying God only knows the future without planning it. How could he know the future if he did not plan it? It is no use trying to establish divine sovereignty by saying we are less than free. How could we be responsible if we were not free?[3]

A BETTER WAY

Each of these approaches has merit, helping to advance our understanding of the nature and purpose of evil. But they each have a serious weakness. To refine our view and address the three basic questions at the beginning of the chapter, three additional affirmations will be put forward.

First, perhaps an astonishing statement: We really cannot know why God allowed evil to enter his universe. We simply do not know how evil is possible if God is God. Although this may be disappointing to admit, should it really be so surprising that we cannot know how the unthinkable happened, how the outrageous became real? Besides, if we did know, we would somehow be able to justify evil. Why did God create a world in which evil would occur? No one knows. Scripture never says.

We do know many things about evil, some of which have been mentioned in the approaches we reviewed. It improves us. It will not last. It is against God. It is the fault of human decision. Much more could be said, but not how it can be compatible with God's purposes. In many instances, the Bible seems to tell us about evil's purpose.[4] Upon careful examination, however, it becomes clear that in every single case, evil was already in the world. God uses it *once it is here*, which is very different from him creating it in the first place.[5] As theologian Henri Blocher puts it,

> No biblical material, studied with care, allows us to retreat from the denunciation of malignity. We may not compromise its rigor by arguing that God makes use of evil and permits it in order to bring about his purposes, for good does not proceed from evil as such, and its connection with the divine purposes is not taught in respect of the first permission, the origin of evil. Evil remains evil: totally, radically, absolutely.[6]

Second, evil is not isolated from God's plan. However it may have got here, it did not surprise him. God does not merely work within the broad contours, but accomplishes absolutely everything according to his plan. "He does as he pleases with the powers of heaven and the peoples of the earth" (Daniel 4:35). God "works out everything in conformity with the purpose of his will" (Ephesians 1:11). This means that whatever else we may say about evil, it is not outside of God's intentions.

This is a remarkable state of affairs—we do not know how evil got here, but we do know that it fits God's purposes. He is in control of the very reality that contradicts him. And somehow he is not guilty, not responsible for evil. The great confessional statements state the mystery succinctly. One of the most articulate is the Westminster Confession of Faith, in the section on *God's Eternal Decree*:

> God from all eternity did, by the most wise and holy counsel of his own will, freely and unchangeably ordain whatsoever comes to pass: yet so, as thereby neither is God the author of sin, nor is violence offered to the will of the creatures, nor is the liberty or contingency of second causes taken away, but rather established (III.1).

The confession confirms two basic realities. One is that God "ordains," that is, determines absolutely everything; whatever happens is "unchangeable." The other is that God does everything justly and with honor; it is by his "wise" and "holy" decision. God is not arbitrary but good. He is not the "author" of sin—it is not of his responsibility—and he honors the integrity and freedom of all creatures. The two realities are asserted but not reconciled. The apparent paradox of God's power and human freedom is not embarrassing for believers, but rather a point of distinction.

The third affirmation about evil is the most important. The Scriptures do not detain us with speculative discourse on the origins of evil but do tell us everything about the solution. Jesus Christ came into the world to overcome evil in all its forms, and does so in two stages. First, he makes atonement for guilt. At the cross, Christ took the sin of the world on his innocent shoulders and received its sentence so that we would not have to. At the resurrection, he triumphed over evil and ushered in a new era in which humanity is forever reconciled to God. Second, gradually now and fully later, evil will be completely eradicated from the universe and a new order will be established in line with God's behest.

Christian apologetics centers on this great truth. We should be willing to engage in honest discussion of the origins and nature of evil but steer others away from unhelpful conjecture, directing them to see things God's way. Only when we look up and understand that God has resolved the problem in his unique way can we begin to have peace. Only when we realize that a God who would go to the extent he did in the sufferings and victory of Christ is a God who will work all things out in the very best way. This may not explain everything about the outrage of evil, such as Auschwitz, AIDS, or the death of a child, but overcomes it. And it gives the greatest mandate possible to engage in the fight against all injustice, disease, and brokenness, knowing that though, "I am suffering as I am, [yet] I am not ashamed, because I know whom I have believed, and am convinced that he is able to guard what I have entrusted to him for that day" (2 Timothy 1:12).

10

FAITH ON ITS
WAY TO ASSURANCE

> Thus, bound with the fetters of an earthly body,
> however much we are shadowed on every side with
> great darkness, we are nevertheless illumined as
> much as need be for firm assurance when, to show
> forth his mercy, the light of God sheds even a little
> of its radiance.
>
> —John Calvin,
> *Institutes of the Christian Religion,* 1559

KEEPING HONEST, KEEPING FAITH

A MAN WITH A DERANGED SON came to Jesus, asking him to heal
the boy if he could. Jesus replied, "Everything is possible for him
who believes." The father then exclaimed, "I believe; help my
unbelief."[1] Faith, as we see in this story, is progressive and varies
by person. With Christian apologetics what matters more than
establishing once-for-all certainty is the ground we are gaining.
Although we have the task of persuading unbelievers of the truth
of the gospel, we need to remember that every assertion does
not necessarily have equal authority. Essentials are clear and
believable, but as we move away from the center we will discover that some matters are less obvious and need to be treated
as tentative.

In this concluding chapter we will explore the matter of
doubt and certainty. All kinds of challenges to Christian faith
can provoke doubts and misgivings: Some involve such issues as

the crusades, world religions, or the problem of evil; others stem from psychological struggles, such as wondering about God's love or his goodness. Our point of view throughout will be to regard faith as dynamic, varying from the minimum needed to enter into relationship with Christ all the way to full persuasion.

HONEST QUESTIONS, HONEST ANSWERS

L'Abri has always had a policy that "honest questions deserve honest answers." Recognizing that no one could claim total honesty, the leaders of l'Abri were committed to take every good question seriously. When I was there, one of the students, a very shy young woman, had a question she thought too dumb to ask. We all knew she wanted to find out how Francis Schaeffer would respond, but the right moment never seemed to appear. Finally she posed her question, something about prayers not being answered. Schaeffer paused, waiting a rather long time to respond. We were tense, wondering what the timid young woman was feeling. Was she thinking that it was far too simplistic for the great theologian? At long last he began to answer, saying that he had to pause and think, because it was the most profound question he had heard in years! He then spoke profoundly for about forty-five minutes, after which the young woman was never afraid to ask a question again.

Giving honest answers to honest questions means more than supplying the resolutions to the issues raised. It also means being forthright and admitting we don't know when the answers are not available. We have already encountered the notion of mystery in regards to the origins of evil and the relation between God's power and human freedom. Another large area that has only partial answers derives from scientific investigation and the Bible.

It often comes as a surprise to laypeople to learn that the archeology of the Holy Land is incomplete when it comes to corroborating the stories in the Bible. There are plenty of open questions, but also abundant evidence to support the events recorded in Scripture. For the thousand years leading up to Christ there is a fair amount of correlation; Egyptian and Assyrian inscriptions support the accounts of the history of Israel. And various recent discoveries add to the evidence. For example, a team led by two Jewish scholars, Joseph Naveh and Avraham Biran, worked in 1993 to excavate Tel Dan in the north of Israel and found chiseled into some igneous rock words that combined, "House of David" and "King of Israel." The date is approximately the ninth century B.C. This find was actually the first evidence outside the Bible of David's existence, dismantling theories that he was a mythical figure.[2] Other finds also support the biblical data, such as ancient clay seals confirming some of Jeremiah's prophecies and quite a few artifacts from the time of Jesus.

On the other side, however, there are not only large gaps where no archeological evidence exists but also apparent conflicts. In the 1950s the British archeologist Kathleen Kenyon undertook extensive excavations at the city of Jericho and concluded that no evidence existed for the destruction of the city some time in the thirteenth century B.C. as described in the Bible. Many subsequent digs appear to confirm her conclusions. In fact, it is generally agreed that the ancient city was decimated some time in the fifteenth century B.C., as were others mentioned in the book of Joshua, such as Ai and Hazor, and that by Joshua's time there was no one there to conquer.

How should apologetics account for the gaps and contradictions? To begin with, we must realize that the science of archeology is far from unequivocal. Research is slow and painstaking and even when a breakthrough occurs, conclusions are usually tentative. Thus the trend to doubt Jericho's conquest could easily be reversed. Some scholars have questioned Kathleen Kenyon's methods, finding evidence of bias in her research. Others have suggested that towns like Jericho and Ai may have been in different locations from their present counterparts or that these cities eroded, which commonly happened during the Middle Bronze period in question.

We also need to underline that a good deal of the biblical teaching, which indeed demands historical accuracy, may not be verifiable by historical research. Much of the biblical story focuses on minor, rather ordinary, figures—whether saints or scoundrels. Elijah, we are told, was "a man just like us" (James 5:17) who did great things through faith in God. The measure of the greatness, however, is usually not in terms of conquest or upheaval nor of events that leave a trail of archeological evidence behind, but of moral progress, ministry, relief to those in need, and piety.

CREATION AND EVOLUTION

The most controversial of the subjects where Bible and science seem to clash is not archeology, but geology, paleontology, and biology. In the nineteenth century this issue was brought to the forefront by a bold theory—evolution. Because the issue of origins is at stake, the question of evolution and creation has understandably generated a great deal of contention. How should Christian apologetics steer the discussion in a healthy direction?

Charles Darwin himself started out desiring to defend the biblical account of creation. His great innovation in his *On the Origin of Species* (1859) was not so much the evolution of the various species but the mechanism of natural selection.[3] The great diversity of species, he argued, occurred over a period of time by such processes as random variation and the struggle for survival. He believed his arguments were compatible with Scripture, because no one but an all-wise God could have devised such a plan. But then in his second book, *The Descent of Man* (1871), he took the bold step of saying that every species, including human beings, could be explained by evolution. An enormous controversy has surrounded these views ever since.

Although many of Darwin's specific theories are no longer accepted, the general contours remain. Has evolution disproved the Bible? Popular books on science and religion, high-profile conflicts such as the Scopes Trial, and the recent debates over high-school textbooks unfortunately give the misleading impression that Christians are obscurantists fighting a forlorn battle against the overwhelming monolith of science.

What does the text of Genesis really say? Does it require six twenty-four–hour days? Although a surface reading lends that impression, many biblical scholars believe it is quite legitimate to consider the Hebrew word for "day" as indicating a period of time. Among other things, they cite the fact that the seventh day never ends (Genesis 2:2). Others believe the structure of Genesis 1 is not chronological but literary because of a poetic correlation between days one and four, two and five, and three and six. Thus they maintain the book is not claiming to set forth a geological time-scheme. Still others believe the text of Genesis should not be forced to make it teach any scientific knowledge at all. As early as 1880, Asa Gray, the Harvard botanist, declared that to hold a conflict between evolution and Genesis is to rely on "extraneous suppositions and forced constructions of language." The two areas, science and Mosaic teaching, were of "different orders."

What Genesis does clearly teach is that God created everything in the universe. Whether over a period of time or succinctly, he is the Creator whose word is sufficient to bring it all forth. It is also clear that human beings were created in a unique way and for a unique purpose. Adam is considered to be the covenant representative of the human race throughout the Bible. To question the historicity of the first man is, among other things, to call into question the analogy that is affirmed between Adam and Christ.[4]

Does the theory of evolution contradict these teachings? Only as a macrotheory grounds everything in a mechanism that works by itself. As a microexplanation there is nothing inherently unbiblical about God's using some kind of process to create. Besides, there are enormous questions in the theories. Most scientists now reject any idea of a smooth process over the millennia, believing that biological change often occurs in sudden fits and starts.

It is best to let the Bible speak on its own terms and not force particular scientific theories out of it. It is best also to let science do its work, occasionally reminding scientists that they cannot claim neutrality. Particular legitimate questions stemming from various discoveries will remain, but new vistas may be opened thanks to science, helping us understand God's world. Again, we will never have the full picture, but can live with the ambiguities when we hold to the biblical teaching: "Now faith is being sure of what we hope for and certain of what we do not see. That is what the ancients were commended for. By faith we understand that the universe was formed at God's command, so that what is seen was not made out of what was visible" (Hebrews 11:1–3).

TWO CRUCIAL REMINDERS

Assurance of faith is far more than having honest questions about big issues, such as science and the Bible, answered honestly. It is more fundamentally a matter of rightly understanding who God is and how we should relate to him.

In the mountain region of Southern France a number of older traditional Huguenot churches have members who come from a long line of faithful believers. Yet in some of those churches an unsettling phenomenon occurs at the time of the Holy Communion—many of the faithful will not come forward to partake. When asked about their reticence they say, "We are not sure we are saved, and we do not dare presume to reenact the sign of belonging to Christ."

These solid believers have probably forgotten that they are saved not because of what *they* might do for God, but because of what *God* has done for them. In chapter 5 of Romans Paul tells his readers that they have peace with God because they have been justified through faith. He is not referring to a feeling of peace, but is saying that God is at peace with us because Christ took the guilt of our condition on himself.

Justification by faith—the great trumpet call of the Protestant Reformation—is a fact, not a feeling. It is a legal status attributed to us by God who simply *declares* it to be so, meaning that we are acquitted and not guilty. Justification has nothing to do with a change in us, but rather one entirely outside us.

This is the first great reminder we need if we are doubting our secure standing with God. If we place our trust and confidence in God through Christ, then it is a most basic fact that we are justified and thus have peace with God. Paul makes two points about our changed status. One is that we are boldly confident to *stand* in the grace of God (5:2). The other is that we actually rejoice in God (5:2, 11)—our assurance is not just a bare mental state of certainty but is emotionally engaging. Knowing what is objectively true because of God's grace and love, we can be more than certain of our relationship to him.

The second great reminder for those whose faith needs strengthening is distinct from the first. If we are justified, Paul tells us, we must take required courses in the school of suffering (5:3). We cannot know all the reasons why we will suffer, but we know that somehow it will be for our benefit. It may be tempting in doing apologetics to skip over the cost of discipleship and avoid Christ's demand for taking up our cross and being willing to give up everything for his sake. But we must honor the inquirer with honest answers to honest questions.

In the school of suffering there are three great degrees, to be earned in sequence. The first is "perseverance" (5:3). When we endure hardship for the sake of our Lord, we begin to learn what no other teacher can impart, the ability to endure. This virtue is notably absent from modern culture—we would rather have the easy pay-off and the pleasurable stimulus than the hard road of daily struggle. But as great athletes know, matches aren't won in one move, but rather one point at a time.

The second degree, once endurance is well in hand, is "character" (5:4). The Greek word here signifies the "ability to pass a test." My father worked for a retired general who exemplified this notion of character. I was with him during a particularly stressful time in the company's life when employees were being laid off and sales were down. When I asked him how he took the pressure, he responded saying that he had been an officer in the Vietnam War and had to make the tough decisions of sending regiments into dangerous territory. The woes of the corporate world did not seem so difficult after that experience. In Paul's terms, he had character.

Finally, the highest degree in the school of suffering is "hope" (5:4–5). As we explored in the passage in 1 Peter, when the New Testament speaks of hope, it means full assurance. And what is underscored in Romans 5 is a hope that does not have any shame or embarrassment attached to it. Furthermore, it is a hope that leads to the same kind of glad feelings that come with justification: "We rejoice in the hope of the glory of God" (5:2).

What the apostle Paul is really saying is that the same God who first justified us will bring us safely through the school of suffering to the place of final victory. We know and can be glad that we will be saved through God's final judgment of the world. Thus the ultimate goal of Christian apologetics is to lead doubters to full assurance of faith by a proper understanding of who God is.

CONCLUSION

Knowing God through faith, then, is the goal of apologetics. Being a Christian and engaging in persuasion is no easier today than it ever was, and is fully effective only when we keep the reality of God in the forefront. By faith we can know that God's intentions for us are good and just, although we cannot always see clearly how this works out. Faith is not an irrational leap, but a basic trust in the One we have every reason to trust. As we grow in our knowledge of God, we grow in our faith. We learn that many issues are resolved here and now, but others will have to wait. God knows every good and sufficient answer for every query, but we do not. Much of what we do not see clearly now will one day be made clear. Far more important than having all the answers, though, is to grow in our trust, so that we will commune with God and fully experience his love. There can be no higher calling.

This is what the LORD says:

"Let not the wise man boast of his wisdom
     or the strong man of his strength
     or the rich man of his riches,
but let him who boasts boast about this:
     that he understands and knows me,
that I am the LORD, who exercises kindness,
     justice and righteousness on earth,
     for in these I delight," declares the LORD.

—Jeremiah 9:23–24

APPENDIX

FOR THOSE WISHING TO READ FURTHER in Christian apologetics, the following volumes will prove useful. They touch on different aspects of the subjects raised in this book, taking the reader deeper into the subject matter. They are by no means written from the same point of view, nor do they agree with all that I have presented. But they will reward careful study and encourage those who want to explore various avenues.

Berger, Peter L. *A Rumor of Angels: Modern Society and the Rediscovery of the Supernatural.* New York: Doubleday, 1969.

Blocher, Henri. *Evil and the Cross.* Downers Grove: InterVarsity Press, 1994.

Clendenin, Daniel B. *Many Gods, Many Lords: Christianity Encounters World Religions.* Grand Rapids: Baker Books, 1995.

Denton, Michael. *Evolution: A Theory in Crisis.* Bethesda: Adler & Adler, 1986.

Dooyeweerd, Herman. *Roots of Western Culture: Pagan, Secular, and Christian Options.* Toronto: Wedge, 1979.

Dyrness, William. *How Does America Hear the Gospel?* Grand Rapids: Eerdmans, 1989.

Evans, James H. Jr. *We Have Been Believers: An African-American Systematic Theology*. Minneapolis: Fortress Press, 1992.

Ford, Kevin Graham. *Jesus for a New Generation*. Downers Grove: InterVarsity Press, 1995.

Frame, John M. *Apologetics to the Glory of God*. Phillipsburgh: Presbyterian & Reformed, 1994.

Gaede, S. D. When Tolerance Is No Virtue: *Political Correctness, Multiculturalism and the Future of Truth and Justice*. Downers Grove: InterVarsity Press, 1993.

Guinness, Os. *God in the Dark: The Assurance of Faith Beyond a Shadow of Doubt*. Wheaton: Crossway, 1996.

————. *The Gravedigger File: Papers on the Subversion of the Modern Church*. Downers Grove: InterVarsity Press, 1983.

Kreeft, Peter. *Between Heaven and Hell*. Downers Grove: Inter-Varsity Press, 1982.

————. *Making Sense out of Suffering*. Ann Arbor: Servant, 1986.

Lewis, C. S. *Mere Christianity*. New York: Macmillan, 1978.

————. *The Problem of Pain*. New York: Macmillan, 1962.

Middleton, J. Richard and Brian J. Walsh: *Truth Is Stranger than It Used to Be: Biblical Faith in a Postmodern Age*. Downers Grove: InterVarsity Press, 1995.

Midgley, Mary. *Evolution as a Religion: Strange Hopes and Stranger Fears*. London: Methuen, 1985.

Monroe, Kelly, ed. *Finding God at Harvard*. Grand Rapids: Zondervan, 1996.

Mouw, Richard. *Distorted Truth: What Every Christian Needs to Know about the Battle for the Mind*. San Francisco: Harper & Row, 1989.

Newbigin, Lesslie. *The Gospel in a Pluralist Society*. Grand Rapids: Eerdmans; Geneva: WCC, 1989.

Neill, Stephen. *Christian Faith and Other Faiths*. Downers Grove: InterVarsity Press, 1984.

Oden, Thomas C. *After Modernity... What?* Grand Rapids: Zondervan , 1990.

Packer, James I. *Knowing Man*. Westchester: Cornerstone, 1979.

Pratt, Richard L. *Every Thought Captive: A Study Manual for the Defense of Christian Truth*. Phillipsburg: Presbyterian & Reformed, 1979.

Schaeffer, Francis A. *Trilogy*. Wheaton: Crossway, 1990.

James W. Skillen: *The Scattered Voice: Christians at Odds in the Public Square*. Grand Rapids: Zondervan, 1990.

Sproul, R. C. *Surprised by Suffering*. Wheaton: Tyndale, 1988.

Toulmin, Stephen. *Cosmopolis: The Hidden Agenda of Modernity*. Chicago: University of Chicago Press, 1990.

Van Til, Cornelius. *Christian Apologetics*. Phillipsburg: Presbyterian & Reformed, 1976

———. *An Introduction to Systematic Theology*. Phillipsburg: Presbyterian & Reformed, 1974.

Wolters, Albert. *Creation Regained: Biblical Basics for a Reformational Worldview*. Grand Rapids: Eerdmans, 1985.

NOTES

Introduction: The Credibility Gap

1. A number of editions of the *Pensées* exist. One of the best English translations is by A. J. Krailsheimer (London: Penguin, 1966). The sayings quoted are 110 and 423 in that edition.

Chapter 1: Today's Unusual Opportunity

1. Just to take one example, there was a confusion between the word *Logos*, which is used at the beginning of John's gospel, and the same Greek word, which meant "universal reason." In this way the apologists identified the *Logos* with Christ. But the meaning of John's *logos* is not based in Greek philosophy, but rooted in the Old Testament teaching on word and revelation. The idea of a universal reason was quite foreign to John.
2. *Rainbows for the Fallen World* is the title of a fine book on aesthetics by Calvin Seerveld (Toronto: Tuppens Press, 1980).
3. See Diogenes Allen, *Christian Belief in a Postmodern World: The Full Wealth of Conviction* (Louisville: Westminster/John Knox, 1989), p. 3.
4. A host of writers has been taking the position that postmodernity is an opportunity for apologetics. Allen in *Christian Belief in a Postmodern World* says that we are finally free from the bonds of rationalism and that Christianity is credible again. See also Paul J. Griffiths, *An Apology for Apologetics* (Maryknoll: Orbis, 1991); Thomas Oden, *After Modernity... What?* (Grand Rapids: Zondervan, 1990); and Brian J. Walsh, "Who Turned Out the

121

Lights? The Light of the Gospel in a Post-Enlightenment Culture," *Faculty Dialogue* 13, 1990, 43–62.

5. François Lyotard, *The Postmodern Condition* (Minneapolis: University of Minnesota Press, 1984), p. xxiv.

6. This would only mean we are in ultramodernity. See Anthony Giddens, *The Consequences of Modernity* (Stanford: Stanford University Press, 1990), p. 53. Using quite different criteria, Jürgen Habermas has also rejected the notion of postmodernity. See Hal Foster, ed., *Postmodern Culture* (London: Pluto, 1983). Using still different norms, Os Guinness critiques the idea. See his *The American Hour* (New York: The Free Press, 1992), p. 129.

Chapter 3: Apostolic Apology

1. See Acts 24:10; 25:8; 26:1; and so on.

2. Here in 1 Peter the reference is clearly judicial as well, at least in good part. Though the letter is written to the Christian church in general, the apostle's immediate audience seems to have been a primarily Gentile church. Peter uses images and themes from the Old Testament extensively, but this probably shows more about his own way of looking at things than the nature of his readership.

3. Edmund P. Clowney, *The Message of First Peter* (Leicester: InterVarsity Press, 1988), pp. 23–24.

4. Luke 12:11; see also 21:14; Matthew 10:19; Mark 13:11.

5. See Edward J. Young, *The Book of Isaiah*, vol. I (Grand Rapids: Eerdmans, 1965), p. 311.

6. See Claude-Bernard Costecalde, *Aux origines du Sacré biblique* (Paris: Letouzey & Ané, 1986).

7. See Matthew 15:1–20.

8. Costecalde, *Aux origines*, p. 147.

9. Intriguingly, the passage from Isaiah goes on to use the metaphor of the rock. As we know, Peter's name, given by Christ, means "rock." It is naturally one of his own favorite metaphors. See, for example, 1 Peter 2:4–8.

10. See 1:3; 1:13; 1:21; 3:5 and so on.

11. The King James translates powerfully, "and hope putteth not to shame."

12. Quoted in Richard J. Mouw, *Uncommon Decency* (Downers Grove, Ill.: InterVarsity, 1992), p. 145.
13. Charles H. Spurgeon, *Sermons*, vol. 42 (London: Passmore & Alabaster, 1896), p. 256. It is only fair to add that Spurgeon was not consistent with his own view. Much of what he stood for was in fact conversant with apologetics.
14. Matthew 16:1–4; see 12:38–42.

Chapter 4: The Larger Biblical Mandate

1. Isaiah 1:18. This word, "reason," (*venivachtah, Niphal imperative, cohortative*), is from a Hebrew word (*YKTh*), meaning to argue, to prove, adjudge, and is closely linked to apologetics. The word *YKTh* is also used in Job 23:7, where he asks for an upright man to present his case.
2. Here the term is *nahneyeti* (*Niphil pretorit*, first person singular, from *ANaH*), meaning respond, answer, testify. The concept is often quasilegal.
3. My emphasis. See also 6:27–30, where the "apologist" is compared to a tester of metals.
4. See Hosea 4:1; 12:2; Micah 6:2; Isaiah 48:1–11; 49:1, 5; 50:1 and following; 55:1 and following; 59:1; and so on.
5. See Job 28:28; Psalm 111:10; Proverbs 1:7.
6. It is likely that Leviathan, the beast of Job 41, is Satan.
7. 1 Corinthians 16:8–9; see also 2 Corinthians 6.
8. 1 Thessalonians 1:5, my emphasis.
9. See 1 Corinthians 2:6 and 10; John 14:15 and following; 15:26.
10. The term for persuasion, *pleirophoreo*, is a strong one. It means to cause a thing to be shown to the full; to fill with conviction or inclination; to give most certain confidence.

Chapter 5: A Rich Palette

1. John Calvin, *Institutes of the Christian Religion*, I.3:1.
2. See Jacques Ellul, *The New Demons* (New York: Seabury, 1975).
3. See the helpful discussion of the universality of religion in Roy Clouser, *The Myth of Religious Neutrality* (Notre Dame: University of Notre Dame Press, 1991), pp. 9–48. For a useful guide to the way religion may be public or private across the

globe, see José Casanova, *Public Religions in the Modern World* (Chicago: University of Chicago Press, 1994).

4. The Greek shows that Paul is not necessarily talking of a past occurrence but one that is ongoing. The American Standard comes closer to the meaning by translating it, "Because that, knowing God, they glorified him not as God. . . ."

5. See Romans 1:16, where Paul calls the gospel "the power of God."

6. See, for example, Romans 1:4; 15:13, 19; 1 Corinthians 2:4; Galatians 3:5.

7. See Romans 4:21; 14:5; Colossians 2:2; 4:12; 2 Timothy 4:5, 17.

8. Frank Morrison, *Who Moved the Stone?* (London: Faber & Faber, 1930).

9. James H. Billington, "Unexpected Joy," *Theology Today* 52/3, 1995, pp. 382–391.

Chapter 6: Initial Barriers

1. All the cases mentioned are real. Occasionally names have been changed for the sake of anonymity.

2. See Erich Auerbach, *Mimesis*, Willard Trask, trans. (Garden City: Anchor Books, 1957), pp. 430 and following.

3. See, for example, *Why I Am Not a Christian and Other Essays of Religion and Related Subjects* (New York: Simon & Schuster, 1957).

Chapter 7: Beyond Belief

1. See *The Fiery Brook: Selected Writings of Ludwig Feuerbach*, Zawar Hanfi, trans. (Garden City: Doubleday, 1972).

2. First published in 1927. See W. D. Roson-Scott, trans. (Garden City: Anchor, 1964).

3. Ibid., pp. 79–80.

4. Since Freud's time the objectivity of science has been severely undermined. Thomas Kuhn, who wrote *The Structure of Scientific Revolutions* (Chicago: University of Chicago Press, 1970), has introduced the notion of the "paradigm shift" into common parlance. His thesis is that new directions in science occur not because we observe the facts better, but because we change the mental rules whereby we solve problems. There has been a good

deal of debate about this kind of theory, but it is safe to say that Freud's simple trust in science is not so widespread as it once was.

Chapter 8: One Way? No Way?

1. See Romans 1 and 2.
2. From the Heidelberg Catechism, 1563.

Chapter 9: The Great Outrage

1. See Marie Moscovici, "La situation du témoin," *La Quinzaine littéraire* No. 675, August 1995, pp. 15–16.
2. The fact that Satan was present in the Garden of Eden to tempt the first couple does not change the argument. It simply pushes the appearance of evil back, to the invisible (created) angelic world, where presumably there was also a fall and a decision to sin.
3. It is important to point out that the essence of freedom is not the power of contrary choice. What makes us free is not that we have options, although we may. In heaven, when we will have no option to choose evil, we will be most free. The essence of our freedom is to be self-determining. We are accountable because it is we who choose, not an external force.
4. King David, for example, was miserable after committing adultery with Bathsheeba and sending her husband to die in a war. In Psalm 32 he recounts, "When I kept silent, my bones wasted away through my groaning all day long. For day and night your hand was heavy upon me. . ." (32:3–4). But this suffering drove him to confess his guilt and find relief (32:5).
5. The Tree of the Knowledge of Good and Evil was in the Garden, but we are not told how. We are told why. It was a test of allegiance to God. Had it been resisted, presumably humanity would have moved from uprightness to eternal bliss. As it is, access to the Tree of Life will be through Christ.
6. Henri Blocher: *Evil and the Cross* (Downers Grove: Inter-Varsity Press, 1994), p. 90.

Chapter 10: Faith on its Way to Assurance

1. Mark 9:14–32. The NRSV translation is more accurate here than the NIV.

2. In 1994 the French archeologist André Lemaire, who had been studying the Mesha Stele at the Louvre Museum, published the results of his findings. The phrase "House of David" occurs there as well, inscribed by an enemy of Israel, King Mesha, a name also found in the Bible.

3. Robert Chambers in his Vestiges of the Natural History of Creation (1844) had earlier affirmed that simpler types gave rise to more complex types through evolution.

4. See Romans 5:12–19; 1 Corinthians 15:22.

WILLIAM EDGAR is Professor of Apologetics at Westminster Theological Seminary in Philadelphia, where he has served on the faculty since 1989. Born in North Carolina, Dr. Edgar has lived much of his life in France and Switzerland. Before coming to Westminster Seminary, he served as a professor of the Faculté Libre de Théologie Réformée in Aix-en-Provence, France, and has been a teacher at the Brunswick School in Greenwich, Connecticut.

Currently he is the managing editor of the *Westminster Theological Journal,* President of the Huguenot Fellowship, Vice-President of the Centre Art et Vie (Marseilles), and serves on the boards of FOCUS and the Greenwood School. Among his writings are *In Spirit and in Truth* and *Taking Note of Music.*

He received a B.A. (in music) from Harvard University, an M.Div. from Westminster Theological Seminary, and a doctorate (in theology) from the Université de Genève in Switzerland. He and his wife have two grown children.